A gift for

_____

from

_____

I Wandered Lonely as a Cloud...

By the same author:

The Book Club Bible: The Definitive Guide That Every Book Club Member Needs (ed.)

I Wandered Lonely as a Cloud...

—⁂—

...and other poems
you half-remember
from school

edited by
ANA SAMPSON

MICHAEL O'MARA BOOKS LIMITED

First published in Great Britain in 2009 by
Michael O'Mara Books Limited
9 Lion Yard
Tremadoc Road
London SW4 7NQ

A CIP catalogue record for this book is available from the British Library.

Papers used by Michael O'Mara Books Limited are natural, recyclable products made
from wood grown in sustainable forests. The manufacturing processes conform to the
environmental regulations of the country of origin.

ISBN: 978-1-84317-394-6

2 3 4 5 6 7 8 9 10

www.mombooks.com

Designed and typeset by www.glensaville.com

Printed and bound in Great Britain by Clays Ltd, St Ives plc

CONTENTS

Introduction

I do not presume to provide a comprehensive overview of poetry in English in this book, or to present a roll call of the finest, or the most seminal, verse. Rather, I hope to take a nostalgic tour of the half-remembered lines and phrases from schooldays, as well as the poems and fragments of poems that we find – sometimes to our own surprise – that we can recite. If anyone tells you that they don't know any poetry – and many happily told me just that – ask them whether the following phrases are familiar: 'the darling buds of May'; 'no country for old men'; 'Laugh, and the world laughs with you'; 'They fuck you up, your mum and dad'; 'The Owl and the Pussy-Cat went to sea.' The wonderful thing about poetry is that we know poetry we don't know we know, if I may put it so confusingly.

Often we don't know that we are familiar with, say, Robert Herrick's 'To the Virgins, to Make Much of Time' until we hear the first line: 'Gather ye rosebuds while ye may.' Sometimes it's just a line in the middle of a poem that catches in the memory: 'Water, water every where, / Nor any drop to drink' from Coleridge's *The Rime of the Ancient Mariner*, or 'To morrow to fresh Woods, and Pastures new' from Milton's *Lycidas*. So I have included here an index of the most famous lines from the poems, whether or not they are the opening lines, so that you can find 'the one that goes . . . '

Early on, I realized uneasily what a subjective selection this would have to be. The poetry that we know depends on our teachers' whims, our parents' tastes, the misery or otherwise of our teenage years, our age, nationality and sometimes our gender, so it is impossible to include everyone's favourites. I apologize wholeheartedly if long-cherished poems do not appear, but I hope that this collection may perhaps inspire you to seek them out elsewhere. As many people as possible were consulted – just ask my poor colleagues and family – to compile a list that would ring bells with the widest readership, and this has led to some surprising omissions. I could find almost nobody, for example, who could quote any Dryden, so the first Poet Laureate is not represented here despite his importance to the story of poetry.

Thematically ordering the poems was impossible, because part of the fun is that a poem rarely speaks to us about a solitary subject. Donne, for example, talks about a flea at the same time as lecturing his too-chaste lover about withholding her evidently considerable charms. So I have elected to place the poets in chronological order, which has thrown up its own odd pleasures as Wilfred Owen, mired in tragedy, is followed by Dorothy Parker rakishly cradling her martini.

Poring over anthologies has been ridiculously good fun, but I found myself greedy for more than the poems. I wanted to remind myself whether a poet had been up to no good with his sister, or whether the poem was inspired by a spat with another writer. Was this verse dedicated to a flesh-and-blood lover? Did readers at the time flock to buy it in their droves, or think it was avant-garde nonsense? I've had a whale of a time finding all this out and it has added immeasurably to my pleasure in the poems. It has also almost certainly upped my chances in pub quizzes. Give me your arm, old toad,* and I hope you have as much fun as I have along the way.

ANA SAMPSON

London, August 2009

---

* A phrase I half-recalled from a school assembly more years ago than I'm happy to admit, without knowing it was from Larkin's 'Toads Revisited'.

ONE
'Shall I compare thee to a summers' day?'

Geoffrey Chaucer (*c.*1343-1400)

Chaucer's father was a London wine seller, and he himself was a working man all his life, including stints as a customs officer, a soldier and a diplomat. His masterpiece *Troilus and Criseyde* is the first English work to use the words 'tragedy' and 'comedy'. He was the first poet to be buried in Poet's Corner in Westminster Abbey, though presumably it wasn't called that at the time.

The Canterbury Tales

We often forget that Chaucer never finished *The Canterbury Tales*, because what we have is such a large fragment. His pilgrims set out for the shrine of Thomas Becket, singing for their supper as the landlord promises a slap-up meal for the best story. Best-loved among them are 'The Miller's Tale', with some excellent fart jokes, and the lusty, merry 'Wife of Bath's Tale'. This extract is from 'The General Prologue'.

Whan that April with his showres soote
The droughte of March hath perced to the roote,
And bathed every veine in swich licour,
Of which vertu engendred is the flowr;
Whan Zephyrus eek with his sweete breeth
Inspired hath in every holt and heeth
The tendre croppes, and the yonge sonne
Hath in the Ram his halve cours yronne,
And smale fowles maken melodye
That sleepen al the night with open ye –
So priketh hem Nature in hir corages –
Thanne longen folk to goon on pilgrimages,

And palmeres for to seeken straunge strondes,
To ferne halwes, couthe in sondry londes;
And specially from every shires ende
Of Engelond to Canterbury they wende,
The holy blisful martyr for to seeke
That hem hath holpen whan that they were seke.

(*His* – its; *soote* – fresh; *swich* – such; *licour* – liquid; *Zephyrus* – the West Wind; *eek* – also; *inspired* – breathed into; *holt* – grove; *heeth* – field; *croppes* – shoots; '*Hath . . . yronne*' – the 'young' sun is only halfway through its course in Aries (the first sign of the zodiac, which the sun enters at the vernal equinox, 20 March); *fowles* – birds; *ye* – eye; *hem* – them; *hir corages* – their hearts; *goon* – go; *palmers* – palmers (far-travelling pilgrims); *ferne* – faraway; *halwes* – shrines; *couthe* – known; *londes* – lands; *holpen* – helped; *seke* – sick.)

Sir Philip Sidney (1554–86)

As Sidney lay mortally wounded at the Battle of Zutphen, it is claimed that he gave his water bottle to another injured soldier, saying 'Thy necessity is yet greater than mine.' This did his reputation as the perfect Elizabethan courtier no harm at all: brave, handsome, and charming, Sidney was adored by his contemporaries and lauded by other poets. He was given a grand send-off as the first commoner to be granted a state funeral.

The Countess of Pembroke's Arcadia

Sidney wanted his prose *Arcadia* destroyed on his death, but his beloved sister Mary, Countess of Pembroke, wisely ignored this. It was vastly popular, and Charles I is reputed to have quoted it on the scaffold.

My True Love Hath My Hart from *The Countess of Pembroke's Arcadia*

My true-love hath my hart, and I have his,
By just exchange, one for the other giv'ne.
I holde his deare, and myne he cannot misse:
There never was a better bargaine driv'ne.

His hart in me, keepes me and him in one,
My hart in him, his thoughtes and senses guides:
He loves my hart, for once it was his owne:
I cherish his, because in me it bides.

His hart his wound receaved from my sight:
My hart was wounded, with his wounded hart,
For as from me, on him his hurt did light,
So still methought in me his hurt did smart:
Both equall hurt, in this change sought our blisse,
My true love hath my hart and I have his.

Verse Drama

I admit that it must seem a trifle remiss to bring together best-loved poetry in the English language, while neglecting the countless examples that appear in plays written in verse. It leaves us with nothing about Marlowe's Helen of Troy – the face that launched a thousand ships – or any passages from Shakespeare. However, this book would have needed twice the number of pages to do such extracts justice, and so, reluctantly, they have had to be omitted. The majority of European drama was written in blank verse for centuries, from the great Greek tragedies onwards. Apart from the grandeur that verse lends to drama, it has the practical advantage of making it easier for actors to remember their lines.

Christopher Marlowe (1564–93)

Marlowe seems more myth than man: we think him a magician, atheist, Catholic, counterfeiter, homosexual and spy, though his life is shrouded in enigmas. We do know he was a brilliant playwright who lit the way for Shakespeare, among others, with his masterly tragedies, including *Dr Faustus*. His death in a pub fight has spawned a number of conspiracy theories, including a tryst with some local lothario gone wrong, or a connection to espionage (he had been employed by the government on some shady business abroad). More prosaically, it is generally thought to have resulted from a simple row over the bill.

The Passionate Shepherd to His Love

In spoilsport Sir Walter Ralegh's 'The Nymph's Reply to the Shepherd', the older poet's heroine deflates Marlowe's starry-eyed rustic, pointing out that the ravages of time and, more threateningly, the British weather will sour love's young dream.

Come live with me and be my love,
And we will all the pleasures prove
That valleys, groves, hills, and fields,
Woods, or steepy mountain yields.

And we will sit upon the rocks,
Seeing the shepherds feed their flocks,
By shallow rivers to whose falls
Melodious birds sing madrigals.

And I will make thee beds of roses
And a thousand fragrant posies,
A cap of flowers, and a kirtle
Embroidered all with leaves of myrtle;

A gown made of the finest wool
Which from our pretty lambs we pull;

Fair lined slippers for the cold,
With buckles of the purest gold;

A belt of straw and ivy buds,
With coral clasps and amber studs:
And if these pleasures may thee move,
Come live with me, and be my love.

The shepherds' swains shall dance and sing
For thy delight each May morning:
If these delights thy mind may move,
Then live with me and be my love.

The Sonnet

The fourteen-line sonnet form originated in thirteenth-century Italy, where it was adopted by Dante and, especially, Petrarch; it takes its name from the Italian for 'little song'. Sir Thomas Wyatt and the Earl of Surrey brought the sonnet to Henry VIII's court, and a distinct, English style emerged. The English sonnet usually has ten syllables per line, employs iambic pentameter, follows the rhyme scheme abab cdcd efef gg, and originally focused on themes of love or religious faith. Shakespeare, in particular, but also Milton, Donne, Wordsworth and Elizabeth Barrett Browning, among many others, wrote memorable sonnets, and Owen employed the form for his anguished 'Anthem for Doomed Youth'.

William Shakespeare (1564–1616)

It's impossible to calculate Shakespeare's legacy, from the phrases he coined to the immortal characters he created. So it is surprising just how little we know about him. The son of a glovemaker from Stratford-upon-Avon, Shakespeare made a name for himself with his crowd-pleasing dramas for the London stage, and he composed some of the most striking and enduring lines ever written. Of his non-dramatic verse, it is his 154 sonnets that most enchant us. Initially circulated privately among friends, the sonnets were published only in 1609 and much neglected until the following century. Now, of his works only *Hamlet* has provoked more critical head-scratching. The first 126 poems are addressed to a mysterious Young Man, and the rest to the equally enigmatic Dark Lady, and there has been endless speculation about their identities. To add to the puzzle, they are dedicated to an unidentified 'Mr W. H.', and we don't even know exactly when they were written.

Sonnet 18

Shall I compare thee to a summer's day?
Thou art more lovely and more temperate:
Rough winds do shake the darling buds of May,
And summer's lease hath all too short a date:
Sometime too hot the eye of heaven shines,
And often is his gold complexion dimm'd:
And every fair from fair sometime declines,
By chance, or nature's changing course untrimm'd;
But thy eternal summer shall not fade,
Nor lose possession of that fair thou ow'st,
Nor shall death brag thou wander'st in his shade,
When in eternal lines to time thou grow'st;
So long as men can breathe, or eyes can see,
So long lives this, and this gives life to thee.

Sonnet 116

Let me not to the marriage of true minds
Admit impediments. Love is not love
Which alters when it alteration finds,
Or bends with the remover to remove:
O, no! it is an ever-fixed mark,
That looks on tempests and is never shaken;
It is the star to every wandering bark,
Whose worth's unknown, although his height be taken.
Love's not Time's fool, though rosy lips and cheeks
Within his bending sickle's compass come;
Love alters not with his brief hours and weeks,
But bears it out even to the edge of doom.
If this be error, and upon me prov'd,
I never writ, nor no man ever lov'd.

The Metaphysical Poets

The poets gathered under this banner – John Donne, Andrew Marvell, George Herbert, Henry Vaughn and a few others – were in fact a disparate group who, despite being contemporaries, did not see themselves as a cohesive 'movement'. However, they share key characteristics: a taste for innovative imagery (such as Donne's flea); an affinity with the preoccupations of the age as science ate into old religious certainties and Civil War convulsed Britain; and a good dollop of wit. Much of their work is moulded by the religious landscape of the time. Luther and Calvin had opened up a direct hotline to God for their followers, free from the clergy's intervention, and religion could never, at this time, be divorced from politics.

John Donne (1572–1631)

Donne eloped with his adored wife Anne without permission from her father or his employer. As a result he was sacked as Secretary to the Great Seal and, briefly, imprisoned. He bemoaned his career suicide in a letter to his wife that read, 'John Donne. Anne Donne. Un-done.' Later, while abroad, he claimed to have seen a vision of Anne – distraught and holding a dead child – at the exact moment that she had suffered a stillbirth. He eventually became Dean of St Paul's Cathedral. He was never free of religious doubt, though he was famed for thunderous sermons. Some of Donne's most famous lines appear in his 'Meditation XVII' rather than his poetry, which includes the passage beginning 'No man is an Island'. In later years Donne rather morbidly posed in a shroud for a portrait, reproduced in marble for the only memorial in St Paul's to have survived the 1666 Great Fire of London.

The Flea

Mark but this flea, and mark in this,
How little that which thou deniest me is;
Me it sucked first, and now sucks thee,
And in this flea our two bloods mingled be;
Thou know'st that this cannot be said
A sin, or shame, or loss of maidenhead,
Yet this enjoys before it woo,
And pampered swells with one blood made of two,
And this, alas, is more than we would do.

O stay, three lives in one flea spare,
Where we almost, nay more than married are.
This flea is you and I, and this
Our marriage bed, and marriage temple is;
Though parents grudge, and you, we are met,
And cloistered in these living walls of jet.
Though use make you apt to kill me,

Let not to that, self-murder added be,
And sacrilege, three sins in killing three.

Cruel and sudden, hast thou since
Purpled thy nail in blood of innocence?
Wherein could this flea guilty be,
Except in that drop which it sucked from thee?
Yet thou triumph'st, and say'st that thou
Find'st not thy self nor me the weaker now;
'Tis true; then learn how false fears be:
Just so much honour, when thou yield'st to me,
Will waste, as this flea's death took life from thee.

Song

Go and catch a falling star,
Get with child a mandrake root,
Tell me where all past years are,
Or who cleft the Devil's foot,
Teach me to hear mermaids singing,
Or to keep off envy's stinging,
And find
What wind
Serves to advance an honest mind.

If thou beest born to strange sights,
Things invisible to see,
Ride ten thousand days and nights,
Till age snow white hairs on thee,
Thou, when thou return'st, wilt tell me
All strange wonders that befell thee,

And swear
No where
Lives a woman true, and fair.

If thou find'st one, let me know,
Such pilgrimage were sweet;
Yet do not, I would not go,
Though at next door we might meet;
Though she were true when you met her,
And last, till you write your letter,
Yet she
Will be
False, ere I come, to two, or three.

Ben Jonson (1572?–1637)

Jonson's elegant epigrams contrast with what we know of his character. He worked as a bricklayer in his youth and was something of a scrapper, killing at least one man in a duel. He was also a legendary drinker who once walked to Scotland to drink a friend's cellar dry in three boozy weeks. Jonson was a prominent London playwright and actor, and rather unlucky to have been a contemporary of Shakespeare, who casts a long shadow. Jonson's poems include moving epitaphs on the deaths of two of his children, country-house poems in which the poet praises his patrons by eulogizing their lovely estates, and masques co-written with the architect Inigo Jones, with whom he later bitterly and publicly fell out.

Song: To Celia

Drink to me only with thine eyes,
And I will pledge with mine;
Or leave a kiss but in the cup,
And I'll not look for wine.
The thirst that from the soul doth rise
Doth ask a drink divine:
But might I of Jove's nectar sup,
I would not change for thine.

I sent thee late a rosy wreath,
Not so much honouring thee,
As giving it a hope that there
It could not withered be.
But thou thereon didst only breathe,
And sent'st it back to me;
Since when it grows and smells, I swear,
Not of itself, but thee.

Robert Herrick (1591–1674)

Rather suspiciously, the infant Herrick's father fell out of a window two days after writing a will, though the courts generously didn't confiscate the family's estate as they did in suicide cases. His support for the Royalist cause during the Civil War lost Herrick his position as vicar of Dean Prior, Devon, but he was reinstated at the Restoration of Charles II. Though he initially found life as a country parson dull, he grew to love Devon. He also had a pet pig, and trained it to drink from a tankard, which must have passed the time.

To the Virgins, to Make Much of Time

Herrick never married, though there is some evidence that he ran off to London with a musician's daughter, and fathered an illegitimate daughter. For a bachelor, his early poems in particular have some fairly racy passages; this *'carpe diem'* (Latin: 'Seize the day!') poem does, however, advise marriage rather than feckless fornication.

Gather ye rosebuds while ye may,
Old time is still a-flying;
And this same flower that smiles today,
Tomorrow will be dying.

The glorious lamp of heaven, the sun,
The higher he's a-getting,
The sooner will his race be run,
And nearer he's to setting.

That age is best which is the first,
When youth and blood are warmer;
But being spent, the worse, and worst
Times still succeed the former.

Then be not coy, but use your time,
And while ye may, go marry;
For having lost but once your prime,
You may forever tarry.

TWO
'To-morrow to fresh Woods and Pastures new'

Edmund Waller (1606–87)

Waller's love poems provide further examples of the '*carpe diem*' genre, instructing young women to relinquish their silly scruples and succumb to the poet's charms. Loyal to the King, Waller tried to maintain London as a Royalist stronghold, but when 'Waller's Plot' was discovered in 1643, he kept his head through the judicious use of bribes and betrayals. He feathered his nest under Cromwell, securing his reinstatement by writing him an obsequious poem – and duly trotted out verses to Charles II at the Restoration in 1660. When the King complained that his poem was inferior to Cromwell's, Waller, ever the consummate politician, assured him that poets write fiction better than they do the truth.

Song

Go lovely Rose,
Tell her that wastes her time and me,
That now she knows
When I resemble her to thee
How sweet and fair she seems to be.

Tell her that's young,
And shuns to have her graces spy'd
That hadst thou sprung
In desarts where no men abide,
Thou must have uncommended dy'd.

Small is the worth
Of beauty from the light retir'd;
Bid her come forth,

Suffer her self to be desir'd,
And not blush so to be admir'd.

Then die that she,
The common fate of all things rare
May read in thee;
How small a part of time they share,
That are so wondrous sweet and fair.

John Milton (1608–74)

Apparently, Milton grumbled that he needed to be 'milked' of poetry after he went blind, which is a not altogether comfortable image. He wrote in support of the Commonwealth until its last gasp in 1659. He also argued in favour of divorce on grounds of incompatibility, a position that was not entirely disinterested as his wife, who was half his age, had fled back to her parents' house weeks into their marriage, although she did later return. At the Restoration Milton was imprisoned, escaping with his life through having loyal friends in high places, among them Andrew **Marvell**. He composed his masterpiece *Paradise Lost* in 1667, though he was by then blind, living in relative poverty, and tainted by a reputation as a dangerous firebrand.

Lycidas [extract]

This elegy for a drowned friend is one of Milton's earliest poems.

Now, Lycidas, the shepherds weep no more;
Henceforth thou art the Genius of the shore,
In thy large recompense, and shalt be good
To all that wander in that perilous flood.
Thus sang the uncouth swain to th'oaks and rills,

While the still morn went out with Sandals gray;
He touched the tender stops of various quills,
With eager thought warbling his Doric lay.
And now the sun had stretched out all the hills,
And now was dropped into the western bay;
At last he rose, and twitched his mantle blue:
To-morrow to fresh woods, and pastures new.

Sonnet XIX: When I Consider How my Light is Spent

This sonnet is an eloquent and moving meditation on Milton's blindness.

When I consider how my light is spent
E're half my days in this dark world and wide,
And that one talent which is death to hide
Lodg'd with me useless, though my Soul more bent
To serve therewith my Maker, and present
My true account, lest he returning chide,
'Doth God exact day-labour, light deny'd?
I fondly ask; but Patience, to prevent
That murmur, soon replies, 'God doth not need
Either man's work or his own gifts; who best
Bear his milde yoak, they serve him best, his State
Is Kingly; thousands at his bidding speed
And post o'er Land and Ocean without rest:
They also serve who only stand and waite.

Paradise Lost [extract]

Samuel Johnson was among *Paradise Lost*'s many admirers, but did admit that 'None ever wished it longer than it is.'

Of Man's First Disobedience, and the fruit
Of that forbidden tree, whose mortal taste
Brought death into the world, and all our woe,
With loss of Eden, till one greater Man
Restore us, and regain the blissful seat,
Sing, Heav'nly Muse, that on the secret top
Of Oreb, or of Sinai, didst inspire
That shepherd who first taught the chosen seed,
In the beginning how the heav'ns and earth
Rose out of Chaos; or if Sion Hill
Delight thee more, and Siloa's brook that flowed
Fast by the oracle of God, I thence
Invoke thy aid to my advent'rous Song,
That with no middle flight intends to soar
Above th' Aonian mount, while it pursues
Things unattempted yet in prose or rhyme.

Richard Lovelace (1618–57)

The aptly named Lovelace was quite the heartbreaker at the glittering Court of Charles I, yet his best-loved poems were written in prison. He served abroad in the military and his beloved, Lucy Sacheverell, married another suitor after poor old Lovelace was wrongly reported to have been killed in action. When the Civil War began, he was incarcerated by Parliament for his Royalist activities, and he died three years too early to see the Restoration of the monarchy.

To Althea, from Prison

When Love with unconfinèd wings
Hovers within my gates,
And my divine Althea brings
To whisper at the grates;
When I lie tangled in her hair
And fettered to her eye,
The gods that wanton in the air
Know no such liberty.

When flowing cups run swiftly round
With no allaying Thames,
Our careless heads with roses bound,
Our hearts with loyal flames;
When thirsty grief in wine we steep,
When healths and draughts go free,
Fishes that tipple in the deep
Know no such liberty.

When, like committed linnets, I
With shriller throat shall sing
The sweetness, mercy, majesty,
And glories of my king;
When I shall voice aloud how good
He is, how great should be,
Enlargèd winds, that curl the flood,
Know no such liberty.

Stone walls do not a prison make,
Nor iron bars a cage;
Minds innocent and quiet take
That for an hermitage;
If I have freedom in my love,

And in my soul am free,
Angels alone, that soar above,
Enjoy such liberty.

Andrew Marvell (1621–78)

Mild-mannered Marvell weathered one of the most turbulent passages in English history, for his career endured through the cavalier Court of Charles I, the Civil War, the Commonwealth and the Restoration. He was best known as a politician during his lifetime, though he did circulate some anonymous satires, one of which the diarist Samuel Pepys read and found 'sharp and so true'. His poetry, which aligns him to a great extent with the metaphysical poets, was published after his death by his housekeeper (who claimed also to have been his secret wife).

To His Coy Mistress

Had we but world enough, and time,
This coyness, Lady, were no crime.
We would sit down, and think which way
To walk, and pass our long love's day.
Thou by the Indian Ganges' side
Shouldst rubies find: I by the tide
Of Humber would complain. I would
Love you ten years before the Flood:
And you should, if you please, refuse
Till the conversion of the Jews.
My vegetable love should grow
Vaster than empires, and more slow.
An hundred years should go to praise
Thine eyes, and on thy forehead gaze.
Two hundred to adore each breast:
But thirty thousand to the rest.

An age at least to every part,
And the last age should show your heart.
For, Lady, you deserve this state;
Nor would I love at lower rate.
But at my back I always hear
Time's wingèd chariot hurrying near:
And yonder all before us lie
Deserts of vast eternity.
Thy beauty shall no more be found,
Nor, in thy marble vault, shall sound
My echoing song: then worms shall try
That long preserved virginity:
And your quaint honour turn to dust,
And into ashes all my lust.
The grave's a fine and private place,
But none I think do there embrace.
Now therefore, while the youthful hue
Sits on thy skin like morning dew,
And while thy willing soul transpires
At every pore with instant fires,
Now let us sport us while we may;
And now, like amorous birds of prey,
Rather at once our time devour,
Than languish in his slow-chapt power.
Let us roll all our strength, and all
Our sweetness, up into one ball:
And tear our pleasures with rough strife,
Thorough the iron gates of life.
Thus, though we cannot make our sun
Stand still, yet we will make him run.

John Bunyan (1628–88)

Bunyan fought in the Parliamentary army during the Civil War but fell foul of the authorities later. After what he claimed was a fairly dissolute youth (he had a reputation for extreme swearing), he was inspired by hearing God's voice and his earthy and passionate manner made him a popular speaker. On the Restoration in 1660, however, the government clamped down on evangelical preachers, and he spent twelve years in Bedford prison. Many of his works were written in jail, including the allegorical *The Pilgrim's Progress* so beloved of the goody-goody March girls in Louisa M. Alcott's novel *Little Women*. On his release he amassed a following of several thousand believers and was affectionately known as 'Bishop Bunyan' by his flock.

Who Would True Valour See

This poem appears in *The Pilgrim's Progress* and in the nineteenth century was set to music as a hymn. A delightful parody can be found in Alan Ahlberg's collection of poems for schoolchildren, *Please Mrs Butler*.

Who would true Valour see
Let him come hither;
One here will Constant be,
Come Wind, come Weather.
There's no *Discouragement*,
Shall make him once *Relent*,
His first avow'd *Intent*,
To be a Pilgrim.

Who so beset him round,
With dismal *Stories*,
Do but themselves Confound;
His Strength the *more* is.
No *Lyon* can him fright,
He'l with a *Gyant Fight*,

But he will have a right,
To be a Pilgrim.

Hobgoblin, nor foul *Fiend,*
Can *daunt* his Spirit:
He knows, he *at the end,*
Shall Life Inherit.
Then Fancies fly away,
He'll fear not what men say,
He'll labour Night and Day,
To be a Pilgrim.

Jonathan Swift (1667–1745)

The Dublin-born Swift is best remembered now for his satirical novel *Gulliver's Travels.* He was popular despite his rather sarcastic temperament, partly because he always lampooned the top strata of society and defended the underdog. A third of his fortune was spent on charitable works. A prolific political journalist, for much of his life he alternated between England and Ireland, eventually being appointed Dean of St Patrick's Cathedral, Dublin, where he was a vocal opponent of English treatment of Ireland. His 'Stella' poems are dedicated to Esther Johnson, though it is unclear whether they married as they seem never to have spent time alone together – perhaps, for Swift, this proved a recipe for a happy union. They were buried side by side.

A Beautiful Young Nymph Going to Bed [extracts]

Swift's song of disgust is a dire warning against 'beer goggles' and feminine artifice, and allegedly caused some early readers to vomit.

Corinna, Pride of *Drury-Lane,*
For whom no Shepherd sighs in vain;
Never did *Covent Garden* boast

So bright a batter'd, strolling Toast;
No drunken Rake to pick her up,
No Cellar where on Tick to sup;
Returning at the Midnight Hour;
Four Stories climbing to her Bow'r;
Then, seated on a three-legg'd Chair,
Takes off her artificial Hair:
Now, picking out a Crystal Eye,
She wipes it clean, and lays it by.
Her Eye-Brows from a Mouse's Hyde,
Stuck on with Art on either Side,
Pulls off with Care, and first displays 'em,
Then in a Play-Book smoothly lays 'em.
Now dextrously her Plumpers draws,
That serve to fill her hollow Jaws.
Untwists a Wire; and from her Gums
A Set of Teeth completely comes.
Pulls out the Rags contriv'd to prop
Her flabby Dugs and down they drop.

. . .

Corinna wakes. A dreadful Sight!
Behold the Ruins of the Night!
A wicked Rat her Plaister stole,
Half eat, and dragg'd it to his Hole.
The Crystal Eye, alas, was miss't;
And *Puss* had on her Plumpers piss'd.
A Pigeon pick'd her Issue-Peas;
And *Shock* her Tresses fill'd with Fleas.
The Nymph, tho' in this mangled Plight,
Must ev'ry Morn her Limbs unite.
But how shall I describe her Arts
To recollect the scatter'd Parts?

Or shew the Anguish, Toil, and Pain,
Of gath'ring up herself again?
The bashful Muse will never bear
In such a Scene to interfere.
Corinna in the Morning dizen'd,
Who sees, will spew; who smells, be poison'd.

Alexander Pope (1688–1744)

As a Catholic, Pope was barred from a political or an academic career and he began hobnobbing with other writers in the fashionable London coffee houses, living by his pen. His major works include *An Essay on Criticism*, which contains the often-quoted line 'a little learning is a dangerous thing'. His mock-heroic verse satire *The Dunciad* is a scathing attack on the dullness of contemporary culture. It offended half of literary London, and Pope was glad of the protection of his dog, Bounce, while out walking after its publication. Perhaps due to his perpetual ill health, he had a habit of falling asleep all over the place – Dr Johnson tells us that he once nodded off at the dinner table while the Prince of Wales held forth about poetry.

The Rape of the Lock [extracts]

Pope based his society satire on a real incident in which the smitten Lord Petre ungallantly helped himself to a lock of Arabella Fermor's hair.

What dire offence from am'rous causes springs,
What mighty contests rise from trivial things,
I sing – This verse to *CARYL*, Muse! is due:
This, ev'n Belinda may VOUCHSAFE to view:
Slight is the subject, but not so the praise,
If She inspire, and He approve my lays.

Say what strange motive, Goddess! could compel
A well-bred Lord t' assault a gentle Belle?

O say what stranger cause, yet unexplor'd,
Could make a gentle Belle reject a Lord?
In tasks so bold, can little men engage,
And in soft bosoms dwells such mighty Rage?
. . .
This Nymph, to the destruction of mankind,
Nourish'd two Locks, which graceful hung behind
In equal curls, and well conspir'd to deck
With shining ringlets the smooth iv'ry neck.
Love in these labyrinths his slaves detains,
And mighty hearts are held in slender chains.
With hairy sprindges we the birds betray,
Slight lines of hair surprise the finny prey,
Fair tresses man's imperial race insnare,
And beauty draws us with a single hair.
. . .
Hither the heroes and the nymphs resort,
To taste awhile the pleasures of a Court;
In various talk th' instructive hours they past,
Who gave the ball, or paid the visit last:
One speaks the glory of the British Queen,
And one describes a charming Indian screen;
A third interprets motions, looks, and eyes;
At ev'ry word a reputation dies.
Snuff, or the fan, supply each pause of chat,
With singing, laughing, ogling, and all that.

Henry Carey (1687?–1743)

Carey was a fearless satirist, and occasionally got into trouble for his plays lampooning the Whig government. Legend has it that he was an illegitimate son of George Savile, first Marquess of Halifax, a claim he neither confirmed nor denied. Perhaps his most enduring legacy, though, is the nickname 'Namby-Pamby', which he coined for the poet and politician Ambrose Philips in a mock-epic including these charming lines: 'Namby-pamby's little rhymes/Little jingles, little chimes/To repeat to little miss,/Piddling ponds of pissy-piss.' Since one of his two wives was called Sarah, of which Sally is a diminutive, his most famous poem may have been inspired by her.

Sally in our Alley [extract]

Of all the girls that are so smart
There's none like pretty Sally;
She is the darling of my heart,
And she lives in our alley.
There is no lady in the land
Is half so sweet as Sally;
She is the darling of my heart,
And she lives in our alley.

Her father he makes cabbage-nets,
And through the streets does cry 'em;
Her mother she sells laces long
To such as please to buy 'em;
But sure such folks could ne'er beget
So sweet a girl as Sally!
She is the darling of my heart,
And she lives in our alley.

THREE
'Earth has not anything to show more fair'

Thomas Gray (1716–71)

Gray loved his time at Eton, writing an *Ode on a Distant Prospect of Eton College* (1747) that includes the famous lines '... where ignorance is bliss / 'Tis folly to be wise'. He continued to shine academically at Cambridge, though he had a morbid phobia of fire and kitted his room out with elaborate safety measures which, predictably, attracted student pranks. After gaining his degree he toured Europe with Horace Walpole, though they quarrelled – probably because Walpole was a party animal and Gray preferred antiquities – and didn't make up for four years. Gray's poetry became hugely popular, though he declined the Laureateship, and lived out a life of quiet scholarship at Cambridge.

Elegy Written in a Country Church Yard [extract]

Gray's masterpiece has bestowed upon the language some of its finest phrases, including 'far from the madding crowd', 'the paths of glory' and 'kindred spirit'. It was composed in the churchyard of Stoke Poges, Buckinghamshire, where he is buried.

The curfew tolls the knell of parting day,
The lowing herd winds slowly o'er the lea,
The ploughman homeward plods his weary way,
And leaves the world to darkness and to me.

Now fades the glimmering landscape on the sight,
And all the air a solemn stillness holds,
Save where the beetle wheels his droning flight,
And drowsy tinklings lull the distant folds;

Save that from yonder ivy-mantled tower
The moping owl does to the moon complain
Of such as, wand'ring near her secret bower,
Molest her ancient solitary reign.

Beneath those rugged elms, that yew-tree's shade,
Where heaves the turf in many a mould'ring heap,
Each in his narrow cell for ever laid,
The rude forefathers of the hamlet sleep.

The breezy call of incense-breathing morn,
The swallow twitt'ring from the straw-built shed,
The cock's shrill clarion, or the echoing horn,
No more shall rouse them from their lowly bed.

For them no more the blazing hearth shall burn,
Or busy housewife ply her evening care:
No children run to lisp their sire's return,
Or climb his knees the envied kiss to share.

Oft did the harvest to their sickle yield,
Their furrow oft the stubborn glebe has broke:
How jocund did they drive their team afield!
How bowed the woods beneath their sturdy stroke!

Let not Ambition mock their useful toil,
Their homely joys, and destiny obscure;
Nor Grandeur hear with a disdainful smile
The short and simple annals of the poor.

The boast of heraldry, the pomp of power,
And all that beauty, all that wealth e'er gave,
Awaits alike th' inevitable hour:
The paths of glory lead but to the grave.

Ode on the Death of a Favourite Cat, Drowned in a Tub of Gold Fishes

This is a salutary tale indeed, though its moral is often misquoted as 'all that glitters is not gold'. Selima was Walpole's cat, and he later displayed the offending receptacle on a pedestal. (A nereid, in Greek mythology, is a sea nymph.)

'Twas on a lofty vase's side,
Where China's gayest art had dyed
The azure flowers that blow;
Demurest of the tabby kind,
The pensive Selima reclined,
Gazed on the lake below.

Her conscious tail her joy declared;
The fair round face, the snowy beard,
The velvet of her paws,
Her coat, that with the tortoise vies,
Her ears of jet, and emerald eyes.
She saw; and purred applause.

Still had she gazed; but 'midst the tide
Two angel forms were seen to glide,
The Genii of the stream:
Their scaly armour's Tyrian hue
Through richest purple to the view
Betrayed a golden gleam.

The hapless Nymph with wonder saw:
A whisker first and then a claw,
With many an ardent wish,
She stretched in vain to reach the prize.
What female heart can gold despise?
What Cat's adverse to fish?

Presumptuous Maid! with looks intent
Again she stretched, again she bent,
Nor knew the gulf between.
(Malignant Fate sat by, and smiled.)
The slipp'ry verge her feet beguiled,
She tumbled headlong in.

Eight times emerging from the flood
She mewed to every watery god,
Some speedy aid to send.
No Dolphin came, no Nereid stirred:
Nor cruel *Tom*, nor *Susan* heard.
A fav'rite has no friend!

From hence, ye Beauties, undeceived,
Know, one false step is ne'er retrieved,
And be with caution bold.
Not all that tempts your wand'ring eyes
And heedless hearts, is lawful prize;
Nor all, that glisters, gold.

Christopher Smart (1722–71)

The son of a steward, Smart married his publisher's stepdaughter, but his father-in-law tended to be controlling of the 'talent', and when the two men fell out Smart was confined to a lunatic asylum for religious mania. It is debatable how mad he actually was, but there was certainly a lively incident of spontaneous prayer in St James's Park, London. (Dr Johnson felt that Smart was simply overly fond of praying and not fond enough of clean linen, and rather approved.)

Jubilate Agno* [Fragment B; extract]

Smart's only company in the asylum was his cat Jeoffrey. This section has been memorably parodied by Wendy Cope: 'For I will consider my lover, who shall remain nameless. / For at the age of 49 he can make the noise of five different makes of lorry changing gear on a hill.'

For I will consider my Cat Jeoffry.
For he is the servant of the Living God
    duly and daily serving him.
For at the first glance of the glory of God in
    the East he worships in his way.
For is this done by wreathing his body seven
    times round with elegant quickness.
For then he leaps up to catch the musk, which
    is the blessing of God upon his prayer.
For he rolls upon prank to work it in.
For having done duty and received blessing
    he begins to consider himself.
For this he performs in ten degrees.
For first he looks upon his fore-paws to see if they are clean.
For secondly he kicks up behind to clear away there.
For thirdly he works it upon stretch with
    the fore-paws extended.
For fourthly he sharpens his paws by wood.
For fifthly he washes himself.
For sixthly he rolls upon wash.
For seventhly he fleas himself, that he may
    not be interrupted upon the beat.
For eighthly he rubs himself against a post.
For ninthly he looks up for his instructions.
For tenthly he goes in quest of food.

---

*   Latin: 'Rejoice in the Lamb.'

For having consider'd God and himself he
    will consider his neighbour.
For if he meets another cat he will kiss her in kindness.
For when he takes his prey he plays with it to give it a chance.
For one mouse in seven escapes by his dallying.

Oliver Goldsmith (1730–74)

Goldsmith saved his energies for socializing, card games and dressing like a dandy during his time at Trinity College, Dublin. Later, he failed to become ordained, worked variously as a doctor, proof-reader and usher, and even busked with his flute before turning to writing. However, he proved his versatility with successful plays including *She Stoops to Conquer*, novels including *The Vicar of Wakefield*, journalism and poetry. A kindly man and a great raconteur, he became a popular – if occasionally exasperating – member of Dr Johnson's circle: Walpole called him 'the inspired idiot' because of the contrast between his elegant writing and his scatterbrained and dissolute lifestyle.

The Deserted Village [extract]

Sweet Auburn! loveliest village of the plain,
Where health and plenty cheered the labouring swain,
Where smiling spring its earliest visit paid,
And parting summer's lingering blooms delayed:
Dear lovely bowers of innocence and ease,
Seats of my youth, when every sport could please,
How often have I loitered o'er thy green,
Where humble happiness endeared each scene;
How often have I paused on every charm,
The sheltered cot, the cultivated farm,

The never-failing brook, the busy mill,
The decent church that topped the neighbouring hill,
The hawthorn bush, with seats beneath the shade,
For talking age and whisp'ring lovers made;
How often have I blessed the coming day,
When toil remitting lent its turn to play,
And all the village train, from labour free,
Led up their sports beneath the spreading tree;
While many a pastime circled in the shade,
The young contending as the old surveyed;
And many a gambol frolicked o'er the ground,
And sleights of art and feats of strength went round;
And still as each repeated pleasure tired,
Succeeding sports the mirthful band inspired;
The dancing pair that simply sought renown
By holding out to tire each other down;
The swain mistrustless of his smutted face,
While secret laughter tittered round the place;
The bashful virgin's side-long look of love,
The matron's glance that would those looks reprove,
These were thy charms, sweet village; sports like these,
With sweet succession, taught e'en toil to please;
These round thy bowers their cheerful influence shed,
These were thy charms – But all these charms are fled.

When Lovely Woman Stoops To Folly

This poem, from *The Vicar of Wakefield*, has attracted numerous parodies, including 'When lovely woman stoops to folly / The evening can be awf'ly jolly.'

When lovely woman stoops to folly,
And finds too late that men betray,
What charm can soothe her melancholy,
What art can wash her guilt away?

The only art her guilt to cover,
To hide her shame from every eye,
To give repentance to her lover,
And wring his bosom, is—to die.

William Cowper (1731–1800)

Cowper (pronounced Cooper) was a sensitive soul, so it's apt that in *Sense and Sensibility* Jane Austen's breathless and silly Marianne Dashwood uses the appreciation of his poetry as an indicator of passion. He coined some of the best-known phrases in the language, including 'God moves in a mysterious way' and 'variety is the spice of life'. Some of his verses are surprisingly merry, although he wrote in part to escape his own demons, notably depression. Cowper was offered a clerk's position in the House of Lords, but the stress of the examination brought on a nervous breakdown. He was institutionalized, and increasingly turned to evangelical religion and obsessing about eternal damnation. After leaving the asylum, he co-wrote the *Olney Hymns*, which includes 'Amazing Grace', with the reformed slaver John Newton.

Verses Supposed to be Written by Alexander Selkirk, during his Solitary Abode in the Island of Juan Fernandez [extract]

Selkirk (1676–1721) was a Scottish sailor who unwisely quarrelled with his captain, and was put ashore on a deserted island, where he lived until his rescue a few years later. His tale also inspired Defoe's *Robinson Crusoe* (1719).

I am monarch of all I survey,
My right there is none to dispute;
From the centre all round to the sea,
I am lord of the fowl and the brute.
Oh, solitude! where are the charms
That sages have seen in thy face?
Better dwell in the midst of alarms,
Than reign in this horrible place.

I am out of humanity's reach,
I must finish my journey alone,
Never hear the sweet music of speech;
I start at the sound of my own.
The beasts, that roam over the plain,
My form with indifference see;
They are so unacquainted with man,
Their tameness is shocking to me.

Society, friendship, and love,
Divinely bestowed upon man,
Oh, had I the wings of a dove,
How soon would I taste you again!
My sorrows I then might assuage
In the ways of religion and truth,
Might learn from the wisdom of age,
And be cheered by the sallies of youth.

Romanticism

It is hard to pin down a definitive date at which romanticism took hold in England – though **Wordsworth** and **Coleridge**'s *Lyrical Ballads* of 1798 is often mooted – but the Romantic movement was devoted to being unfettered, so perhaps the lack of a definitive date is appropriate. Tumultuous revolutions were toppling kings, and artists were freer than ever before to write for themselves and the new readership that the expansion of the press was bringing them, instead of for noble patrons.

Romantic writing prioritized new values, and imagination, inspiration and emotion took centre stage. In a reaction to the urban Augustan age that had gone before, the Romantics were drawn to wild places and felt themselves to be outsiders, as their greatest creations were: *Frankenstein*'s sad monster, Coleridge's Ancient Mariner and **Byron**'s defiant heroes among them. The Lakeland poets – Wordsworth, Coleridge and Southey – who lived and wrote in the Lake District are those most closely associated with the movement.

William Blake (1757–1827)

As a child Blake saw a tree filled with angels in Peckham Rye, south-east London, and he later claimed to have witnessed a fairy's funeral procession. His only formal education was in art, and he illustrated his poems with extraordinary, now iconic, images. In religion, as in politics, he was passionately unorthodox and sketched out his own mythic schemes of belief. As students down the ages will testify, he enjoyed befuddling the reader: 'That which can be made Explicit to the Idiot is not worth my care.' Blake married the illiterate Catherine Boucher and taught her to read and to assist him. They were once seen naked reading *Paradise Lost* to each other in the summerhouse. He died singing.

The Tyger

Tyger! Tyger! burning bright
In the forests of the night,
What immortal hand or eye
Could frame thy fearful symmetry?

In what distant deeps or skies
Burnt the fire of thine eyes?
On what wings dare he aspire?
What the hand dare seize the fire?

And what shoulder, & what art,
Could twist the sinews of thy heart?
And when thy heart began to beat,
What dread hand? & what dread feet?

What the hammer? what the chain?
In what furnace was thy brain?
What the anvil? what dread grasp
Dare its deadly terrors clasp?

When the stars threw down their spears,
And water'd heaven with their tears,
Did he smile his work to see?
Did he who made the Lamb make thee?

Tyger! Tyger! burning bright
In the forests of the night,
What immortal hand or eye
Dare frame thy fearful symmetry?

And did those feet in ancient time (Jerusalem)

England's best-loved hymn is based on a poem that appeared in the preface to Blake's epic poem *Milton*. It is the unofficial anthem of the Women's Institutes, and the official one of the England cricket team.

And did those feet in ancient time,
Walk upon England's mountains green:
And was the holy Lamb of God
On England's pleasant pastures seen?

And did the Countenance Divine
Shine forth upon our clouded hills?
And was Jerusalem builded here
Among these dark Satanic Mills?

Bring me my Bow of burning gold:
Bring me my Arrows of desire:
Bring me my Spear: O clouds unfold!
Bring me my Chariot of fire.

I will not cease from Mental Fight,
Nor shall my Sword sleep in my hand
Till we have built Jerusalem
In England's green & pleasant Land.

Robert Burns (1759–96)

Robbie (or Rabbie) Burns's early poems were an immediate success and the literary establishment (rather patronizingly) lauded him as a 'natural' poet because he drew on Scots traditions and dialect, and was self-educated. He was an important influence on the Romantic movement, but spent most of his life in penury. His Scots poems and songs include 'Auld Lang Syne', while his 'Address to a Haggis' is read over that dish at Burns Night suppers all over the world each 25

January, the poet's birthday. He is of course the national poet of Scotland, where he is often referred to simply as 'the Bard'. He also fathered a platoon of illegitimate children, though he eventually settled (more or less) in Dumfries with his wife and worked as an exciseman. He devoted many years to collecting Scottish folk songs, for which he proudly refused a fee despite struggling financially. He also liked a dirty ditty, and circulated lewd, and at that time unpublishable, rhymes to entertain his friends.

A Red, Red Rose

O, my Luve's like a red, red rose,
That's newly sprung in June:
O, my Luve's like the melodie,
That's sweetly played in tune.
As fair art thou, my bonie lass,
So deep in luve am I,
And I will luve thee still, my dear,
Till a' the seas gang dry.

Till a' the seas gang dry, my dear,
And the rocks melt wi' the sun!
And I will luve thee still, my dear,
While the sands o' life shall run.
And fare-thee-weel, my only Luve,
And fare-thee-weel a while!
And I will come again, my Luve,
Tho' it were ten-thousand mile.

William Wordsworth (1770–1850)

By the last decade of his life the rural idylls Wordsworth depicted were in many places already being gobbled up by Victorian industrialization. How did the young iconoclast, fired up by the French Revolution, whose poems peppered with 'farmyard' language shocked critics, end up as the eminent Poet Laureate? His reputation helped: he was the least scandal-ridden of the racy Romantics by a long shot (the fact that he had an illegitimate daughter was hidden for a hundred years), as well as the longest lived. Wordsworth's vast (though variable) output was studied in schools during his lifetime, and tourists flocked to his beloved Lakes hoping to glimpse him striding about.

I Wandered Lonely As A Cloud

Here at last loyal Dorothy Wordsworth must get some credit: it was she who recorded the image of a sea of daffodils in her diary after one of the siblings' endless hikes. 'Diminutive Dolly' lived with her brother most of his life. She cried for a day when he married, though she continued to live with the newlyweds afterwards. (One can only imagine what the new Mrs Wordsworth made of this.)

I wandered lonely as a cloud
That floats on high o'er vales and hills,
When all at once I saw a crowd,
A host, of golden daffodils;
Beside the lake, beneath the trees,
Fluttering and dancing in the breeze.

Continuous as the stars that shine
And twinkle on the milky way,
They stretched in never-ending line
Along the margin of a bay:
Ten thousand saw I at a glance,
Tossing their heads in sprightly dance.

The waves beside them danced; but they
Out-did the sparkling waves in glee:
A poet could not but be gay,
In such a jocund company:
I gazed – and gazed – but little thought
What wealth the show to me had brought:

For oft, when on my couch I lie
In vacant or in pensive mood,
They flash upon that inward eye
Which is the bliss of solitude;
And then my heart with pleasure fills,
And dances with the daffodils.

Composed Upon Westminster Bridge, September 3, 1802

Earth has not anything to show more fair:
Dull would he be of soul who could pass by
A sight so touching in its majesty:
This City now doth, like a garment, wear
The beauty of the morning; silent, bare,
Ships, towers, domes, theatres, and temples lie
Open unto the fields, and to the sky;
All bright and glittering in the smokeless air.
Never did sun more beautifully steep
In his first splendour, valley, rock, or hill;
Ne'er saw I, never felt, a calm so deep!
The river glideth at his own sweet will:
Dear God! the very houses seem asleep;
And all that mighty heart is lying still!

Samuel Taylor Coleridge (1772–1834)

In 1794 Coleridge met Robert Southey, and together they cooked up a half-baked plan to settle in Pennsylvania and found an artists' colony. Around this time they paired off with the Fricker sisters, Sara and Edith, though Coleridge's marriage to the former failed and she ultimately moved in with the Southeys. He later fell hopelessly in love with Sara Hutchinson, who would become, anagrammatically, the 'Asra' of his poems, and complimented her hair so fervently that she began to wear a cap. A brilliant but troubled man, Coleridge was chided throughout his life for rarely seeing anything to completion. He collaborated with **Wordsworth** on the revolutionary *Lyrical Ballads*, but developed a taste for laudanum dissolved in fine brandy, and ended up half-crippled mentally and financially by his addiction, leading to a rift lasting many years between the two poets.

The Rime of the Ancient Mariner [extracts]

At sea the mariner and his fellow crew members were cursed because he shot an albatross. He is the only survivor of the voyage and continues to atone for his guilt by bothering partygoers.

It is an ancient Mariner,
And he stoppeth one of three.
'By thy long grey beard and glittering eye,
Now wherefore stopp'st thou me?

The Bridegroom's doors are opened wide,
And I am next of kin;
The guests are met, the feast is set:
May'st hear the merry din.'

He holds him with his skinny hand,
'There was a ship,' quoth he.
'Hold off! unhand me, greybeard loon!'
Eftsoons his hand dropt he.

He holds him with his glittering eye--
The Wedding-Guest stood still,
And listens like a three years' child:
The Mariner hath his will.

. . .

Day after day, day after day,
We stuck, nor breath nor motion:
As idle as a painted ship
Upon a painted ocean.

Water, water, everywhere,
And all the boards did shrink;
Water, water, everywhere,
Nor any drop to drink.

The very deep did rot: O Christ!
That ever this should be!
Yea, slimy things did crawl with legs
Upon the slimy sea.

About, about, in reel and rout
The death-fires danced at night;
The water, like a witch's oils,
Burnt green, and blue and white.

And some in dreams assurèd were
Of the spirit that plagued us so;
Nine fathom deep he had followed us
From the land of mist and snow.

And every tongue, through utter drought,
Was withered at the root;
We could not speak, no more than if
We had been choked with soot.

Ah! well a-day! what evil looks
Had I from old and young!
Instead of the cross, the Albatross
About my neck was hung.

. . .

Farewell, farewell! but this I tell
To thee, thou Wedding-Guest!
He prayeth well, who loveth well
Both man and bird and beast.

He prayeth best, who loveth best
All things both great and small;
For the dear God who loveth us,
He made and loveth all.'

The Mariner, whose eye is bright,
Whose beard with age is hoar,
Is gone: and now the Wedding-Guest
Turned from the bridegroom's door.

He went like one that hath been stunned,
And is of sense forlorn:
A sadder and a wiser man,
He rose the morrow morn.

Kubla Khan, or, A Vision in a Dream. A Fragment [extracts]

Coleridge's most famous work is, characteristically, only a fragment because his opium reverie was interrupted by that troublesome 'person from Porlock'.

In Xanadu did Kubla Khan
A stately pleasure-dome decree:
Where Alph, the sacred river, ran
Through caverns measureless to man
Down to a sunless sea.

So twice five miles of fertile ground
With walls and towers were girdled round:
And there were gardens bright with sinuous rills,
Where blossomed many an incense-bearing tree;
And here were forests ancient as the hills,

. . .

The shadow of the dome of pleasure
Floated midway on the waves;
Where was heard the mingled measure
From the fountain and the caves.

It was a miracle of rare device,
A sunny pleasure-dome with caves of ice!
A damsel with a dulcimer
In a vision once I saw:
It was an Abyssinian maid,
And on her dulcimer she played,
Singing of Mount Abora.
Could I revive within me
Her symphony and song,
To such a deep delight 'twould win me,

That with music loud and long,
I would build that dome in air,
That sunny dome! those caves of ice!
And all who heard should see them there,
And all should cry, Beware! Beware!
His flashing eyes, his floating hair!
Weave a circle round him thrice,
And close your eyes with holy dread,
For he on honey-dew hath fed,
And drunk the milk of Paradise.

Charles Lamb (1775–1834)

The 'Lambs of London' were devoted to each other. Charles's sister Mary suffered from episodes of insanity and, during one such breakdown, killed their mother. He cared for Mary for the rest of his life: when the madness descended they would walk to the asylum arm in arm, carrying a straitjacket and weeping. Despite these setbacks, they collaborated to produce *Tales from Shakespeare*, and presided over a literary salon that attracted the most dazzling minds of the day, including **Wordsworth** and **Coleridge**. Charles was a legendary drinker because it relieved his stammer, and was much loved by his circle of friends despite a caustic tongue when provoked by the pretentious. Remarkably, Mary died long after him, at the then considerable age of eighty-two.

Parental Recollections

This poem is often credited, under the title 'A Child', to Mary Lamb.

A child's a plaything for an hour;
Its pretty tricks we try
For that or for a longer space—
Then tire, and lay it by.

But I knew one that to itself
All seasons could control;
That would have mock'd the sense of pain
Out of a grievèd soul.

Thou straggler into loving arms,
Young climber-up of knees,
When I forget thy thousand ways
Then life and all shall cease.

The Old Familiar Faces

Where are they gone, the old familiar faces?

I had a mother, but she died, and left me
Died prematurely in a day of horrors—
All, all are gone, the old familiar faces.

I have had playmates, I have had companions
In my days of childhood, in my joyful school-days;
All, all are gone, the old familiar faces.

I have been laughing, I have been carousing,
Drinking late, sitting late, with my bosom cronies;
All, all are gone, the old familiar faces.

I loved a love once, fairest among women:
Closed are her doors on me, I must not see her –
All, all are gone, the old familiar faces.

I have a friend, a kinder friend has no man;
Like an ingrate, I left my friend abruptly;
Left him, to muse on the old familiar faces.

Ghost-like I paced round the haunts of my childhood;
Earth seemed a desert I was bound to traverse,
Seeking to find the old familiar faces.

Friend of my bosom, thou more than a brother,
Why wert not thou born in my father's dwelling!
So might we talk of the old familiar faces,

How some they have died, and some they have left me,
And some are taken from me; all are departed;
All, all are gone, the old familiar faces.

Clement C. Moore (1779–1863)

Moore was such an unlikely figure to have 'invented' the American Christmas that
there are some conspiracy theories surrounding the authorship of 'A Visit from
St Nicholas'. An academic whose previous works were heavy tomes on Hebrew,
legend has it that he composed his only famous poem to entertain his children
during a sleigh ride through Greenwich Village on Christmas Eve 1822, basing
jolly St Nicholas on their coachman.

Account of a Visit from St Nicholas

'Twas the night before Christmas, when all through the house
Not a creature was stirring, not even a mouse;
The stockings were hung by the chimney with care,
In hopes that St Nicholas soon would be there;
The children were nestled all snug in their beds,
While visions of sugar plums danced in their heads,
And mamma in her 'kerchief, and I in my cap,
Had just settled our brains for a long winter's nap,
When out on the lawn there arose such a clatter,
I sprang from the bed to see what was the matter.

Away to the window I flew like a flash,
Tore open the shutters, and threw up the sash.
The moon on the breast of the new fallen snow,
Gave a luster of mid-day to objects below;
When, what to my wondering eyes should appear,
But a minature sleigh, and eight tiny reindeer,
With a little old driver, so lively and quick,
I knew in a moment it must be St Nick.
More rapid than eagles his coursers they came,
And he whistled, and shouted, and call'd them by name,
'Now! Dasher! now, Dancer! now, Prancer and Vixen!
'On, Comet! on, Cupid! on, Dunder and Blitzem!
'To the top of the porch! To the top of the wall!
'Now dash away! Dash away! Dash away all!'
As dry leaves that before the wild hurricane fly,
When they meet with an obstacle, mount to the sky;
So up to the housetop the coursers they flew,
With the sleigh full of toys, and St Nicholas, too.
And then in a twinkling, I heard on the roof
The prancing and pawing of each little hoof.
As I drew in my head, and was turning around,
Down the chimney St Nicholas came with a bound.
He was dressed all in fur, from his head to his foot,
And his clothes were all tarnish'd with ashes and soot;
A bundle of toys he had flung on his back,
And he looked like a peddler just opening his pack.
His eyes – how they twinkled – his dimples how merry!
His cheeks were like roses, his nose like a cherry;
His droll little mouth was drawn up like a bow,
And the beard of his chin was as white as the snow;
The stump of a pipe he held tight in his teeth,
And the smoke it encircled his head like a wreath;

He had a broad face, and a little round belly,
That shook when he laughed, like a bowlful of jelly.
He was chubby and plump, a right jolly old elf,
And I laughed when I saw him, in spite of myself;
A wink of his eye and a twist of his head
Soon gave me to know I had nothing to dread.
He spoke not a word, but went straight to his work,
And filled all the stockings; then turned with a jerk,
And laying his finger aside of his nose,
And giving a nod, up the chimney he rose;
He sprang to his sleigh, to his team gave a whistle,
And away they all flew, like the down of a thistle;
But I heard him exclaim, ere he drove out of sight,
'Happy Christmas to all, and to all a good night!'

Leigh Hunt (1784–1859)

Hunt got into hot water for writing that the Prince Regent (later George IV) – who was fond of throwing wildly decadent parties – was a libertine, and was imprisoned for two years. The sentence wasn't too arduous, however, as his cell had rose-patterned wallpaper and a little garden, and he was allowed a piano and plenty of visitors. He was constantly in debt, squandering the loans of friends including **Shelley**. Good-natured and optimistic, Dickens took him as a model for Harold Skimpole in *Bleak House*.

Rondeau (Jenny Kissed Me)

Jenny kissed me when we met,
Jumping from the chair she sat in;
Time, you thief, who love to get
Sweets into your list, put that in!
Say I'm weary, say I'm sad,

Say that health and wealth have missed me;
Say I'm growing old, but add,
Jenny kissed me.

George Gordon, Lord Byron (1788–1824)

Byron came from a long line of wicked aristocratic adventurers. He was dazzlingly handsome, despite a club foot and a tendency to chubbiness. Women were not deterred, however: Lady Caroline Lamb called him 'mad, bad and dangerous to know', and allegedly had herself delivered to him naked on a silver platter. He embarked on a scandalous relationship with his half-sister Augusta Leigh, and his marriage to the rather dull 'Annabella' unsurprisingly collapsed. He fled the controversy and held court in Italy, bedding hundreds of women and frantically writing racy poetry. After the publication of *Childe Harold's Pilgrimage* Byron awoke one morning and found himself famous – later, infamous – throughout Europe. He developed the idea of the Byronic hero: a complicated, mysterious and, of course, good-looking sort unfettered by social conventions, though his later work, especially *Don Juan*, was a little too steamy for the public's palate. Byron loved to travel, especially to anywhere dangerous, and fought for the Greeks, to whom he is a national hero, against the Turkish. He died of a fever during a storm at Lepanto, and his heart is buried in Greece.

She Walks in Beauty

Byron wrote this poem during his honeymoon, when his wife and he were still affectionately calling each other 'Pippin' (her) and 'Dear Duck' (him). No doubt she thought of other things to call him later on, when he threatened her with a gun while she was pregnant, and took up with his half-sister.

She walks in beauty, like the night
Of cloudless climes and starry skies;
And all that's best of dark and bright

Meet in her aspect and her eyes:
Thus mellowed to that tender light
Which heaven to gaudy day denies.

One shade the more, one ray the less,
Had half impaired the nameless grace
Which waves in every raven tress,
Or softly lightens o'er her face;
Where thoughts serenely sweet express
How pure, how dear their dwelling-place.

And on that cheek, and o'er that brow,
So soft, so calm, yet eloquent,
The smiles that win, the tints that glow,
But tell of days in goodness spent,
A mind at peace with all below,
A heart whose love is innocent!

Percy Bysshe Shelley (1792 – 1822)

Shelley came from solid, conservative aristocratic stock, though he became a radical in his life and writing. He eloped with the sixteen-year-old Harriet Westbrook, then three years later scandalized society further by running off with Mary Godwin; his first marriage had already collapsed by then. Mary would later write the horror classic *Frankenstein* (1818) after they had scared each other silly with ghost stories in Switzerland. Having married, the Shelleys lived mostly in Italy, where their circle included **Byron**. Shelley was an idealist, and advocated vegetarianism, free love and atheism. He was drowned in Italy, and his bloated corpse was burnt on a pyre by his devoted friends. Mary took the charred heart back to England to be buried, and Shelley's ashes were interred in Rome's Protestant Cemetery – which presumably would have upset his atheist principles, had he known.

Ozymandias

I met a traveller from an antique land
Who said: Two vast and trunkless legs of stone
Stand in the desert. Near them, on the sand,
Half sunk, a shattered visage lies, whose frown,
And wrinkled lip, and sneer of cold command,
Tell that its sculptor well those passions read
Which yet survive, stamped on these lifeless things,
The hand that mocked them and the heart that fed.
And on the pedestal these words appear:
'My name is Ozymandias, king of kings:
Look on my works, ye Mighty, and despair!'
Nothing beside remains. Round the decay
Of that colossal wreck, boundless and bare
The lone and level sands stretch far away.

To a Skylark [extracts]

Hail to thee, blithe Spirit!
Bird thou never wert,
That from Heaven, or near it,
Pourest thy full heart
In profuse strains of unpremeditated art.

Higher still and higher
From the earth thou springest
Like a cloud of fire;
The blue deep thou wingest,
And singing still dost soar, and soaring ever singest.

In the golden light'ning
Of the sunken sun,
O'er which clouds are bright'ning,

Thou dost float and run,
Like an unbodied joy whose race is just begun.

The pale purple even
Melts around thy flight;
Like a star of Heaven,
In the broad daylight
Thou art unseen, but yet I hear thy shrill delight,
. . .
Teach me half the gladness
That thy brain must know,
Such harmonious madness
From my lips would flow
The world should listen then – as I am listening now.

Felicia Dorothea Hemans (1793–1835)

Hemans's work was widely anthologized and often learnt by heart. Having seen her brothers off to the Peninsular Wars and married an Irish army officer – though he did rather caddishly leave her to raise their five sons alone – Hemans often wrote on heroic, patriotic subjects. Her poems have been more or less affectionately parodied, most notably by Spike Milligan, whose pithy version of her most famous poem ran: 'The boy stood on the burning deck / Whence all but he had fled – / The twit!'

Casabianca

Set during the Battle of the Nile in 1798, this poem tells the tale of the heroic young son of Casabianca, a French captain. Although generations of schoolchildren have dutifully learnt it, unquestioning filial obedience did its hero no good at all.

The boy stood on the burning deck
Whence all but he had fled;

The flame that lit the battle's wreck
Shone round him o'er the dead.

Yet beautiful and bright he stood,
As born to rule the storm –
A creature of heroic blood,
A proud, though child-like form.

The flames rolled on – he would not go
Without his father's word;
That father, faint in death below,
His voice no longer heard.

He called aloud: – 'Say, Father, say
If yet my task is done?'
He knew not that the chieftain lay
Unconscious of his son.

'Speak, Father!' once again he cried,
'If I may yet be gone!'
And but the booming shots replied,
And fast the flames rolled on.

Upon his brow he felt their breath,
And in his waving hair,
And looked from that lone post of death
In still yet brave despair;

And shouted but once more aloud,
'My Father! must I stay?'
While o'er him fast, through sail and shroud,
The wreathing fires made way.

They wrapt the ship in splendour wild,
They caught the flag on high,

And streamed above the gallant child
Like banners in the sky.

There came a burst of thunder sound –
The boy – oh! where was he?
Ask of the winds that far around
With fragments strew'd the sea! –

With mast, and helm, and pennon fair,
That well had borne their part,
But the noblest thing which perished there
Was that young faithful heart!

John Keats (1795–1821)

Keats was the humbly born wunderkind who produced some of the most beautiful poetry in English between the ages of eighteen and twenty-six, when he died of consumption in Rome. He was engaged to Fanny Brawne, and after his death she remained in mourning for twelve years: Keats was a predictably hard romantic act to follow. **Byron** blamed Keats's early death on snooty reviews calling him one of the 'Cockney School', but nursing his brother through fatal tuberculosis and then rushing off for a strenuous and soggy tour of the Lake District were the true culprits. **Shelley**'s *Adonais* is a tribute, and helped cement Keats's poetic image as the youthful, tragically doomed literary superstar.

On First Looking into Chapman's Homer

Some of Keats's more churlish peers criticized him for failing to read Homer in the original Greek, and whinged that he had mixed up 'stout Cortez', who discovered Mexico, with Balboa, the first European to sail to the Pacific from the New World. Still, the poem was written in just a morning, which seems a morning pretty well spent.

Much have I travelled in the realms of gold,
And many goodly states and kingdoms seen;
Round many western islands have I been
Which bards in fealty to Apollo hold.
Oft of one wide expanse had I been told
That deep-browed Homer ruled as his demesne;
Yet did I never breathe its pure serene
Till I heard Chapman speak out loud and bold:
Then felt I like some watcher of the skies
When a new planet swims into his ken;
Or like stout Cortez when with eagle eyes
He stared at the Pacific – and all his men
Looked at each other with a wild surmise –
Silent, upon a peak in Darien.

La Belle Dame sans Merci: A Ballad

O what can ail thee, knight-at-arms,
Alone and palely loitering?
The sedge has wither'd from the lake,
And no birds sing.

O what can ail thee, knight-at-arms,
So haggard and so woe-begone?
The squirrel's granary is full,
And the harvest's done.

I see a lily on thy brow,
With anguish moist and fever dew,
And on thy cheeks a fading rose
Fast withereth too.

I met a lady in the meads,
Full beautiful – a faery's child,

Her hair was long, her foot was light,
And her eyes were wild.

I made a garland for her head,
And bracelets too, and fragrant zone;
She looked at me as she did love,
And made sweet moan.

I set her on my pacing steed,
And nothing else saw all day long,
For sidelong would she bend, and sing
A faery's song.

She found me roots of relish sweet,
And honey wild, and manna-dew,
And sure in language strange she said –
'I love thee true.'

She took me to her elfin grot,
And there she wept, and sighed fill sore,
And there I shut her wild wild eyes
With kisses four.

And there she lullèd me asleep
And there I dreamed – Ah! woe betide! –
The latest dream I ever dreamt
On the cold hill side.

I saw pale kings and princes too,
Pale warriors, death-pale were they all;
They cried – 'La Belle Dame sans Merci
Hath thee in thrall!'

I saw their starved lips in the gloam,
With horrid warning gapèd wide,

And I awoke and found me here,
On the cold hill's side.

And this is why I sojourn here
Alone and palely loitering,
Though the sedge is withered from the lake,
And no birds sing.

To Autumn [extract]

Season of mists and mellow fruitfulness,
Close bosom-friend of the maturing sun,
Conspiring with him how to load and bless
With fruit the vines that round the thatch-eves run;
To bend with apples the mossed cottage-trees,
And fill all fruit with ripeness to the core;
To swell the gourd, and plump the hazel shells
With a sweet kernel; to set budding more,
And still more, later flowers for the bees,
Until they think warm days will never cease,
For Summer has o'er-brimmed their clammy cells.

FOUR
'Yours is the Earth and everything that's in it'

Ralph Waldo Emerson (1803–82)

The Sage of Concord, Massachusetts, Emerson was ordained as a Unitarian pastor but later resigned, having found his faith sorely tested by the death of his first wife from tuberculosis in 1831. He remarried in 1835, to Lydia Jackson, whom he addressed as 'Lidian'; she always called him 'Mr Emerson'. Emerson was admired for his kindliness, good sense, and passionate oratory. He scandalized Harvard by denying the divinity of God in a lecture, but they got over it eventually: the Emerson Hall was built there in 1900.

Concord Hymn

By the rude bridge that arched the flood,
Their flag to April's breeze unfurled,
Here once the embattled farmers stood
And fired the shot heard round the world.

The foe long since in silence slept;
Alike the conqueror silent sleeps;
And Time the ruined bridge has swept
Down the dark stream which seaward creeps.

On this green bank, by this soft stream,
We set to-day a votive stone;
That memory may their deed redeem,
When, like our sires, our sons are gone.

Spirit, that made those heroes dare
To die, and leave their children free,

Bid Time and Nature gently spare
The shaft we raise to them and Thee.

Elizabeth Barrett Browning (1806–61)

Elizabeth Barrett's father supported her early literary endeavours – but forbade any of his children to marry. Always sickly, Elizabeth became a recluse and an invalid. She continued to publish poems that sold like hot cakes and were praised by critics, and the young **Robert Browning** – six years her junior – wrote to her: 'I love these books with all my heart – and I love you too.' They eloped in secret to Italy. Her father never forgave her. During their lifetimes Elizabeth was a far greater celebrity than her husband, and she was even a contender for the post of Poet Laureate. She died in Robert's arms in Florence.

Sonnet 43

How do I love thee? Let me count the ways.
I love thee to the depth and breadth and height
My soul can reach, when feeling out of sight
For the ends of Being and ideal Grace.
I love thee to the level of every day's
Most quiet need, by sun and candlelight.
I love thee freely, as men strive for Right;
I love thee purely, as they turn from Praise.
I love thee with the passion put to use
In my old griefs, and with my childhood's faith.
I love thee with a love I seemed to lose
With my lost saints, – I love thee with the breath,
Smiles, tears, of all my life! – and, if God choose,
I shall but love thee better after death.

Henry Wadsworth Longfellow (1807–82)

Longfellow's poems were bestsellers in his own time, though he has achieved the status of a slightly guilty pleasure since. He numbered among New England's 'Fireside Poets', so called because their verses were easy to learn and recite due to their musical rhythms, and were written to be shared by families. Longfellow was tragically unlucky in love. His first wife, Mary, died young, and his second, Frances, burnt to death while using sealing wax on a letter. He grew his bushy beard to hide the burn scars he sustained while trying to save her.

A Psalm of Life [extract]

Lives of great men all remind us
We can make our lives sublime,
And, departing, leave behind us
Footprints on the sands of time;

Footprints, that perhaps another,
Sailing o'er life's solemn main,
A forlorn and shipwrecked brother,
Seeing, shall take heart again.

Let us, then, be up and doing,
With a heart for any fate;
Still achieving, still pursuing,
Learn to labour and to wait.

Hiawatha's Sailing (from *The Song of Hiawatha*, Part VII) [extract]

'Give me of your bark, O Birch-tree!
Of your yellow bark, O Birch-tree!
Growing by the rushing river,
Tall and stately in the valley!
I a light canoe will build me,

Build a swift Cheemaun for sailing,
That shall float upon the river,
Like a yellow leaf in Autumn,
Like a yellow water-lily!
'Lay aside your cloak, O Birch-tree!
Lay aside your white-skin wrapper,
For the Summer-time is coming,
And the sun is warm in heaven,
And you need no white-skin wrapper!'
Thus aloud cried Hiawatha
In the solitary forest,
By the rushing Taquamenaw,
When the birds were singing gaily,
In the Moon of Leaves were singing,
And the sun, from sleep awaking,
Started up and said, 'Behold me!
Gheezis, the great Sun, behold me!'
And the tree with all its branches
Rustled in the breeze of morning,
Saying, with a sigh of patience,
'Take my cloak, O Hiawatha!'

Edgar Allen Poe (1809–40)

Poor old Poe died in poverty, despite his lack of self-doubt: he called 'The Raven' 'the greatest poem that was ever written'. Poe was orphaned at three and it is no surprise that he suffered night terrors as a child; drink and depression haunted him all his life. He married his thirteen year-old cousin Virginia who died from tuberculosis aged only twenty-four. Her bones fell into the hands of an early biographer of Poe, who displayed them to lucky dinner guests until they were finally reburied with those of her husband.

The Raven [extracts]

Once upon a midnight dreary, while I
    pondered, weak and weary,
Over many a quaint and curious volume of forgotten lore –
While I nodded, nearly napping, suddenly
    there came a tapping,
As of some one gently rapping, rapping at my chamber door –
''Tis some visitor,' I muttered, 'tapping at my chamber door –
Only this and nothing more.'

Ah, distinctly I remember it was in the bleak December,
And each separate dying ember wrought
    its ghost upon the floor.
Eagerly I wished the morrow; – vainly I had sought to borrow
From my books surcease of sorrow –
    sorrow for the lost Lenore –
For the rare and radiant maiden whom
    the angels name Lenore –
Nameless *here* for evermore.

. . .

Open here I flung the shutter, when,
    with many a flirt and flutter,
In there stepped a stately Raven of the saintly days of yore.
Not the least obeisance made he; not a
    minute stopped or stayed he;
But, with mien of lord or lady, perched
    above my chamber door –
Perched upon a bust of Pallas just above my chamber door –
Perched, and sat, and nothing more.

. . .

'Prophet!' said I, 'thing of evil! – prophet still, if bird or devil! –
By that Heaven that bends above us – by

    that God we both adore –

Tell this soul with sorrow laden if, within the distant Aidenn,
It shall clasp a sainted maiden whom the angels name Lenore –
Clasp a rare and radiant maiden, whom

    the angels name Lenore.'

Quoth the raven 'Nevermore.'

'Be that word our sign of parting, bird or

    fiend!' I shrieked, upstarting –

'Get thee back into the tempest and the

    Night's Plutonian shore!

Leave no black plume as a token of that

    lie thy soul hath spoken!

Leave my loneliness unbroken! – quit the bust above my door!
Take thy beak from out my heart, and take

    thy form from off my door!'

Quoth the raven 'Nevermore.'

And the raven, never flitting, still is sitting, *still* is sitting
On the pallid bust of Pallas just above my chamber door;
And his eyes have all the seeming of a demon's that is dreaming,
And the lamp-light o'er him streaming

    throws his shadow on the floor;

And my soul from out that shadow that

    lies floating on the floor

Shall be lifted – nevermore!

Pallas – Athene, also known as Pallas Athene (and, to the Romans, as Minerva), in
Greek mythology the goddess of wisdom; *Aidenn* – a place name invented by Poe,
possibly as an echo of Eden, and so a metaphor for Paradise; *Plutonian* – pitch dark,
black (Pluto, also known as Hades, being the Greek god of the Underworld).

Edward FitzGerald (1809–83)

FitzGerald was a great eccentric. A vegetarian who disliked vegetables and often lived on bread and butter, he claimed his whole family was mad including himself, but protested that at least he was aware of it. Fortunately he was wealthy enough to devote his time to literature, music and writing charming letters that have proved invaluable to subsequent literary biographers. His first anonymous translation of *The Rubáiyát* was widely ignored until Swinburne and **Rossetti** discovered and praised it.

The Rubáiyát of Omar Khayyám [extracts]

Omar Khayyám (1048–1123) was a twelfth-century Persian poet, mathematician and astronomer. It has been written that the Persian quatrain (the *ruba'i*) was inspired by the joyful exclamations of an excited child, though FitzGerald isn't scrupulously faithful in either his extremely free translation or rhyme scheme.

I

Awake! for Morning in the Bowl of Night
Has flung the Stone that puts the Stars to Flight:
 And Lo! the Hunter of the East has caught
The Sultán's Turret in a Noose of Light.

II

Dreaming when Dawn's Left Hand was in the Sky
I heard a voice within the Tavern cry,
'Awake, my Little ones, and fill the Cup
Before Life's Liquor in its Cup be dry.'

VII

Come, fill the Cup, and in the fire of Spring
The Winter-garment of Repentance fling:
The Bird of Time has but a little way
To fly—and Lo! the Bird is on the Wing.

XII

Here with a Loaf of Bread beneath the Bough,
A Flask of Wine, a Book of Verse—and Thou
Beside me singing in the Wilderness—
And Wilderness is Paradise enow,

XXVI

Oh, come with old Khayyám, and leave the Wise
To talk; one thing is certain, that Life flies;
One thing is certain, and the Rest is Lies ;
The Flower that once has blown for ever dies.

LI

The Moving Finger writes; and, having writ,
Moves on: nor all thy Piety nor Wit
Shall lure it back to cancel half a Line,
Nor all thy Tears wash out a Word of it.

LII

And that inverted Bowl we call The Sky,
Whereunder crawling coop't we live and die,
Lift not thy hands to It for help—for it
Rolls impotently on as Thou or I.

LVII

Oh, Thou, who didst with Pitfall and with Gin
Beset the Road I was to wander in,
Thou wilt not with Predestination round
Enmesh me, and impute my Fall to Sin?

LXXI

And much as Wine has play'd the Infidel,
And robb'd me of my Robe of Honour—well,
I often wonder what the Vintners buy
One half so precious as the Goods they sell.

LXXIII

Ah Love! could thou and I with Fate conspire
To grasp this sorry Scheme of Things entire,
Would not we shatter it to bits—and then
Re-mould it nearer to the Heart's Desire!

LXXVI

Ah, Moon of my Delight who know'st no wane,
The Moon of Heav'n is rising once again:
How oft hereafter rising shall she look
Through this same Garden after me—in vain!

LXXV

And when Thyself with shining Foot shall pass
Among the Guests Star-scatter'd on the Grass,
And in thy joyous Errand reach the Spot
Where I made one—turn down an empty Glass!

Alfred, Lord Tennyson (1809–92)

After Shakespeare, Tennyson is the most quoted writer in *The Oxford Dictionary of Quotations*, and he bequeathed us phrases including 'Nature, red in tooth and claw' and ''Tis better to have loved and lost / Than never to have loved at all.' At Cambridge he became a close friend of Arthur Henry Hallam, who was later engaged to Tennyson's sister, but died, aged just twenty-two, before they could marry. Hallam's death devastated him, and he worked on his elegy, *In Memoriam A. H. .H*, for seventeen years. It was an immediate hit with critics and readers, including Prince Albert, after whose death Queen Victoria turned to it for comfort in her widow's weeds.

Tennyson became the longest serving Poet Laureate, and was created a baron in 1884. A few crackly recordings of the poet declaiming his poetry survive, though it has been alleged that they might be clearer had the wax cylinders not been stored next to a radiator.

The Lady of Shalott [extracts]

William Holman Hunt (1827–1910) was among several artists to paint subjects drawn from the poem, though Tennyson was irritated by Hunt tangling his Lady in her tapestry because he hadn't specified this in the verse.

On either side the river lie
Long fields of barley and of rye,
That clothe the wold and meet the sky;
And thro' the field the road runs by
To many-towered Camelot;
And up and down the people go,
Gazing where the lilies blow
Round an island there below,
The island of Shalott.

Willows whiten, aspens quiver,
Little breezes dusk and shiver
Thro' the wave that runs for ever
By the island in the river
Flowing down to Camelot.
Four grey walls, and four grey towers,
Overlook a space of flowers,
And the silent isle imbowers
The Lady of Shalott.

By the margin, willow veiled,
Slide the heavy barges trailed
By slow horses; and unhailed
The shallop flitteth silken-sailed
Skimming down to Camelot:
But who hath seen her wave her hand?
Or at the casement seen her stand?
Or is she known in all the land,
The Lady of Shalott?

Only reapers, reaping early
In among the bearded barley,
Hear a song that echoes cheerly
From the river winding clearly,
Down to towered Camelot:
And by the moon the reaper weary,
Piling sheaves in uplands airy,
Listening, whispers, ''Tis the fairy
Lady of Shalott.'

There she weaves by night and day
A magic web with colours gay.
She has heard a whisper say,
A curse is on her if she stay
To look down to Camelot.
She knows not what the curse may be,
And so she weaveth steadily,
And little other care hath she,
The Lady of Shalott.

. . .

His broad clear brow in sunlight glowed;
On burnished hooves his war-horse trode;

From underneath his helmet flowed
His coal-black curls as on he rode,
As he rode down to Camelot.
From the bank and from the river
He flashed into the crystal mirror,
'Tirra lirra,' by the river
Sang Sir Lancelot.

She left the web, she left the loom,
She made three paces thro' the room,
She saw the water-lily bloom,
She saw the helmet and the plume,
She looked down to Camelot.
Out flew the web and floated wide;
The mirror cracked from side to side;
'The curse is come upon me,' cried
The Lady of Shalott.

The Charge of the Light Brigade

Traditionally, while the girls were sniggering at the Lady's curse coming upon her,
the boys were being fed on this improving tale of a disastrous military engagement
during the Crimean War of 1854–6. A report in *The Times* inspired Tennyson over
breakfast and he wrote these verses in minutes.

Half a league, half a league,
Half a league onward,
All in the valley of Death
Rode the six hundred.
'Forward, the Light Brigade!
Charge for the guns!' he said;
Into the valley of Death
Rode the six hundred.

'Forward, the Light Brigade!'
Was there a man dismayed?
Not tho' the soldier knew
Some one had blundered:
Their's not to make reply,
Their's not to reason why,
Their's but to do and die:
Into the valley of Death
Rode the six hundred.

Cannon to right of them,
Cannon to left of them
Cannon in front of them
Volleyed and thundered;
Stormed at with shot and shell,
Boldly they rode and well,
Into the jaws of Death,
Into the mouth of Hell
Rode the six hundred.

Flashed all their sabres bare,
Flashed as they turned in air
Sabring the gunners there,
Charging an army, while
All the world wondered:
Plunged in the battery-smoke
Right thro' the line they broke;
Cossack and Russian
Reeled from the sabre-stroke
Shattered and sundered.
Then they rode back, but not
Not the six hundred.

Cannon to right of them,
Cannon to left of them,
Cannon behind them
Volleyed and thundered;
Stormed at with shot and shell,
While horse and hero fell,
They that had fought so well
Came thro' the jaws of Death,
Back from the mouth of Hell,
All that was left of them,
Left of six hundred.

When can their glory fade?
O the wild charge they made!
All the world wondered.
Honour the charge they made!
Honour the Light Brigade,
Noble six hundred!

Maud [extract]

Come into the garden, Maud,
For the black bat, night, has flown,
Come into the garden, Maud,
I am here at the gate alone;
And the woodbine spices are wafted abroad,
And the musk of the rose is blown.
For a breeze of morning moves,
And the planet of Love is on high,
Beginning to faint in the light that she loves
On a bed of daffodil sky,

To faint in the light of the sun she loves,
To faint in his light, and to die.

Crossing the Bar

Tennyson composed this poem near the end of his long life, and it has the flavour of an elegy. The 'bar' to which the poem refers is a sandbar at the mouth of a harbour or estuary, which vessels can only cross once the tide has risen.

Sunset and evening star,
And one clear call for me!
And may there be no moaning of the bar,
When I put out to sea,

But such a tide as moving seems asleep,
Too full for sound and foam,
When that which drew from out the boundless deep
Turns again home.

Twilight and evening bell,
And after that the dark!
And may there be no sadness of farewell,
When I embark;

For tho' from out our bourne of Time and Place
The flood may bear me far,
I hope to see my Pilot face to face
When I have crost the bar.

Edward Lear (1812–88)

Lear suffered from epilepsy – which he termed 'the Demon' – and depression – 'the Morbids'. He was also rather ugly, though happy to lampoon his own odd appearance ('His nose is remarkably big . . . His beard it resembles a wig'). He became one of the world's best-loved nonsense writers. Lear was also a talented artist and gave Queen Victoria drawing lessons, though he found Court etiquette understandably confusing, and she was almost certainly not amused. He also popularized the limerick, notably through his *Book of Nonsense*, published in 1846. There has been some speculation that his verses were written by his patron the Earl of Derby, 'Lear' being an anagram of 'Earl'.

The Owl and the Pussy-cat

'The Owl and the Pussy-cat' was inspired by Lear's tailless cat Foss, whom he adored so much that, on moving, he had his new house built as a replica of the old to make the move easier on the cat. A 'runcible spoon' is a nonsense device, and simply celebrates the deliciously absurd sound of the word: Lear includes runcible cats, geese and hats in other works.

The Owl and the Pussy-cat went to sea
In a beautiful pea-green boat,
They took some honey, and plenty of money,
Wrapped up in a five-pound note.
The Owl looked up to the stars above,
And sang to a small guitar,
'O lovely Pussy! O Pussy, my love,
What a beautiful Pussy you are,
You are,
You are!
What a beautiful Pussy you are!'

Pussy said to the Owl, 'You elegant fowl!
How charmingly sweet you sing!
O let us be married! too long we have tarried:
But what shall we do for a ring?'
They sailed away, for a year and a day,
To the land where the Bong-tree grows,
And there in a wood a Piggy-wig stood,

With a ring at the end of his nose,
His nose,
His nose,
With a ring at the end of his nose.

'Dear Pig, are you willing to sell for one shilling
Your ring?' Said the Piggy, 'I will.'
So they took it away, and were married next day
By the Turkey who lives on the hill.
They dinèd on mince, and slices of quince,
Which they ate with a runcible spoon;
And hand in hand, on the edge of the sand,
They danced by the light of the moon,
The moon,
The moon,
They danced by the light of the moon.

Robert Browning (1812–89)

Poor Robert was known as 'Mrs Browning's husband' after he and Elizabeth eloped in defiance of her overprotective father, because she was the better-known writer, although he has now claimed his position as one of the great Victorian poets. His epic poem *The Ring and the Book* was hugely popular, and in later years Browning gathered both loyal readers and critical praise. There were dissenters, however: Oscar **Wilde** remarked that the trouble with the novelist George Meredith was that he was a sort of prose Browning – adding that, then again, so was Browning.

Home-Thoughts, from Abroad

Oh, to be in England
Now that April's there,
And whoever wakes in England
Sees, some morning, unaware,

That the lowest boughs and the brushwood sheaf
Round the elm-tree bole are in tiny leaf,
While the chaffinch sings on the orchard bough
In England—now!

And after April, when May follows,
And the whitethroat builds, and all the swallows!
Hark, where my blossomed pear-tree in the hedge
Leans to the field and scatters on the clover
Blossoms and dewdrops—at the bent spray's edge—
That's the wise thrush; he sings each song twice over,
Lest you should think he never could recapture
The first fine careless rapture!
And though the fields look rough with hoary dew,
All will be gay when noontide wakes anew
The buttercups, the little children's dower
—Far brighter than this gaudy melon-flower!

Arthur Hugh Clough (1819–61)

The son of a Liverpool cotton merchant, Clough befriended Matthew **Arnold**
at Oxford University, and Arnold wrote 'Thyrsis' in memory of his friend at his
death. Clough's career was in education, though he resigned his fellowship at the
Anglican Oriel College, Oxford, due to the religious doubts that inspired much of
his poetry. Yet despite wrestling with his faith, Clough was usually a jolly sort.

Say not the Struggle Naught Availeth

This poem was famously quoted, in a radio broadcast of April 1941, by Winston
Churchill, who hoped that it would help to entice the then neutral United States
into joining the Allied cause.

Say not the struggle naught availeth,
The labour and the wounds are vain,

The enemy faints not, nor faileth,
And as things have been, they remain.

If hopes were dupes, fears may be liars;
It may be, in yon smoke concealed,
Your comrades chase e'en now the fliers,
And, but for you, possess the field.

For while the tired waves, vainly breaking,
Seem here no painful inch to gain,
Far back through creeks and inlets making
Comes, silent, flooding in, the main.

And not by eastern windows only,
When daylight comes, comes in the light,
In front the sun climbs slow, how slowly,
But westward, look, the land is bright.

Charles Kingsley (1819–75)

A country parson and marine biology enthusiast, Kingsley is best remembered for his children's novel *The Water-Babies*. He was hugely popular with his flock, despite a serious smoking habit that saw him hiding pipes in bushes around the parish in case he needed a tobacco hit while out visiting. He also, although his parishioners presumably didn't know it, enjoyed a mildly kinky sex life with his wife, Fanny.

Young and Old

When all the world is young, lad,
And all the trees are green;
And every goose a swan, lad,
And every lass a queen;
Then hey for boot and horse, lad,

And round the world away;
Young blood must have its course, lad,
And every dog his day.

When all the world is old, lad,
And all the trees are brown;
And all the sport is stale, lad,
And all the wheels run down;
Creep home, and take your place there,
The spent and maimed among:
God grant you find one face there,
You loved when all was young.

Walt Whitman (1819–92)

Whitman worked on his masterpiece, *Leaves of Grass*, throughout his life. He is America's greatest nineteenth-century poet, and his original voice came to speak for that emerging melting-pot nation. Whitman was affected and inspired by his service as a hospital volunteer during the Civil War, scribbling blood-spattered notes for future reference. The sexual references in his poetry caused some critical commotion, with the *Boston Intelligencer* shrilling that the author must be 'some escaped lunatic' deserving of the lash. However, Whitman became a master publicist – he cheekily quoted **Emerson** on an early book cover without his permission. He remained a rustic and somewhat wild figure all his life: one visitor found only a tin cup, a bowl and a spoon in his kitchen. Abraham Lincoln greatly inspired Whitman: they often passed each other in the street with a courteous bow. The President's assassination devastated the poet and was the catalyst for these verses.

O Captain! My Captain!

O Captain! my Captain! our fearful trip is done,
The ship has weathered every rack, the prize we sought is won,

The port is near, the bells I hear, the people all exulting,
While follow eyes the steady keel, the vessel grim and daring;
But O heart! heart! heart!
O the bleeding drops of red,
Where on the deck my Captain lies,
Fallen cold and dead.

O Captain! my Captain! rise up and hear the bells;
Rise up – for you the flag is flung – for you the bugle trills,
For you bouquets and ribboned wreaths –
    for you the shores a-crowding,
For you they call, the swaying mass, their eager faces turning;
Here Captain! dear father!
This arm beneath your head!
It is some dream that on the deck
You've fallen cold and dead.

My Captain does not answer, his lips are pale and still,
My father does not feel my arm, he has no pulse nor will.
The ship is anchored safe and sound, its
    voyage closed and done,
From fearful trip the victor ship comes in with object won;
Exult O shores, and ring O bells!
But I, with mournful tread,
Walk the deck my Captain lies,
Fallen cold and dead.

When Lilacs Last in the Dooryard Bloom'd [extracts]

When lilacs last in the dooryard bloom'd,
And the great star early droop'd in the western sky in the night,
I mourn'd, and yet shall mourn with ever-returning spring.

Ever-returning spring, trinity sure to me you bring,

Lilac blooming perennial and drooping star in the west,
And thought of him I love.

O powerful western fallen star!
O shades of night – O moody, tearful night!
O great star disappear'd – O the black murk that hides the star!
O cruel hands that hold me powerless – O helpless soul of me!
O harsh surrounding cloud that will not free my soul.

. . .

Coffin that passes through lanes and streets,
Through day and night with the great cloud darkening the land,
With the pomp of the inloop'd flags with
    the cities draped in black,
With the show of the States themselves as
    of crepe-veil'd women standing,
With processions long and winding and
    the flambeaus of the night,
With the countless torches lit, with the silent
    sea of faces and the unbared heads,
With the waiting depot, the arriving
    coffin, and the sombre faces,
With dirges through the night, with the thousand
    voices rising strong and solemn,
With all the mournful voices of the dirges
    pour'd around the coffin,
The dim-lit churches and the shuddering organs
    – where amid these you journey,
With the tolling bells' perpetual clang,
Here, coffin that slowly passes,
I give you a sprig of lilac.

. . .

Passing the visions, passing the night,
Passing, unloosing the hold of my comrades' hands,
Passing the song of the hermit bird and
    the tallying song of my soul,
Victorious song, death's outlet song, yet
    varying ever-altering song,
As low and wailing, yet clear the notes, rising
    and falling, flooding the night,
Sadly sinking and fainting, as warning and
    warning, and yet again bursting with joy,
Covering the earth and filling the spread of the heaven,
As that powerful psalm in the night I heard from recesses,
Passing, I leave thee lilac with heart-shaped leaves,
I leave thee there in the door-yard,
    blooming, returning with spring.

I cease from my song for thee,
From my gaze on thee in the west, fronting
    the west, communing with thee,
O comrade lustrous with silver face in the night.

Julia Ward Howe (1819–1910)

In part to escape her strictly Calvinist father, Julia Ward married in haste. Her much older husband forbade her to write, hoping she would make a tractable housewife. She was fluent in seven languages, a student of philosophy, and rather more stubborn than he had hoped, and their marriage was sometimes tempestuous as a result. In later years she focused her formidable energies on women's suffrage, living to the ripe old age of ninety-one. In 1870 she proclaimed the first Mothers' Day, and nobody (especially her children) dared to argue.

The Battle-Hymn of the Republic

Ward Howe was active in the Union cause during the American Civil War, and composed these new words to the popular tune of 'John Brown's Body'.

Mine eyes have seen the glory of the coming of the Lord:
He is trampling out the vintage where the
    grapes of wrath are stored;
He hath loosed the fateful lightning of His terrible swift sword:
His truth is marching on.
Glory! Glory! Hallelujah! Glory! Glory! Hallelujah!
Glory! Glory! Hallelujah! His truth is marching on.

I have seen Him in the watch fires of a hundred circling camps,
They have builded Him an altar in the
    evening dews and damps;
I can read His righteous sentence by the dim and flaring lamps:
His day is marching on.
Glory! Glory! etc.

I have read a fiery gospel writ in burnished rows of steel:
'As ye deal with my contemners, so with
    you my grace shall deal;
Let the Hero, born of woman, crush the serpent with His heel,
Since God is marching on.'
Glory! Glory! etc.

He has sounded forth the trumpet that shall never call retreat;
He is sifting out the hearts of men before His judgement seat:
Oh, be swift, my soul, to answer Him! Be jubilant, my feet!
Our God is marching on.
Glory! Glory! etc.

In the beauty of the lilies Christ was born across the sea,
With a glory in his bosom that transfigures you and me:

As he died to make men holy, let us die to make men free,
While God is marching on.
Glory! Glory! etc.

Matthew Arnold (1822–88)

Matthew's father, Dr Thomas Arnold, was the famous reforming headmaster of Rugby School. At Oxford University Arnold junior made a name for himself as something of a dandy. It was only when he fell in love, and needed to prove that he had prospects, that he finally settled into the position of Schools Inspector, rattling around provincial Britain on the newborn railway network; he was also Professor of Poetry at Oxford for ten years from 1857. Most of his poetry was written during his younger years – he once said that after his thirtieth birthday he felt 'three parts iced over'.

Dover Beach

'Dover Beach' was begun during Arnold's honeymoon in 1851, but was not published until sixteen years later.

The sea is calm to-night.
The tide is full, the moon lies fair
Upon the straits; – on the French coast the light
Gleams and is gone; the cliffs of England stand,
Glimmering and vast, out in the tranquil bay.
Come to the window, sweet is the night-air!

Only, from the long line of spray
Where the sea meets the moon-blanch'd land,
Listen! you hear the grating roar
Of pebbles which the waves draw back, and fling,
At their return, up the high strand,

Begin, and cease, and then again begin,
With tremulous cadence slow, and bring
The eternal note of sadness in.

Sophocles long ago
Heard it on the Ægæan, and it brought
Into his mind the turbid ebb and flow
Of human misery; we
Find also in the sound a thought,
Hearing it by this distant northern sea.

The Sea of Faith
Was once, too, at the full, and round earth's shore
Lay like the folds of a bright girdle furl'd.
But now I only hear
Its melancholy, long, withdrawing roar,
Retreating, to the breath
Of the night-wind, down the vast edges drear
And naked shingles of the world.

Ah, love, let us be true
To one another! for the world, which seems
To lie before us like a land of dreams,
So various, so beautiful, so new,
Hath really neither joy, nor love, nor light,
Nor certitude, nor peace, nor help for pain;
And we are here as on a darkling plain
Swept with confused alarms of struggle and flight,
Where ignorant armies clash by night.

William Allingham (1824 – 1889)

Allingham started out in that least poetic of careers: as a customs officer. In 1863 he moved to England from his birthplace in County Donegal, Ireland, and edited *Fraser's Magazine*, knocking about with many of the literary lions of London, among them D. G. **Rossetti**, Carlyle and **Tennyson**. His diaries ooze with intriguing insights into this circle.

The Fairies [extract]

Up the airy mountain
Down the rushy glen,
We daren't go a-hunting
For fear of little men;
Wee folk, good folk,
Trooping all together;
Green jacket, red cap,
And white owl's feather!

Down along the rocky shore
Some make their home,
They live on crispy pancakes
Of yellow tide-foam;
Some in the reeds
Of the black mountain lake,
With frogs for their watch-dogs,
All night awake.

Dante Gabriel Rossetti (1828–82)

Rossetti is perhaps best remembered as a painter and founder member of the Pre-Raphaelite Brotherhood. As his adoption of the name suggests, he was obsessed with Dante and his doomed passion for Beatrice, and he himself was always on the lookout for 'stunners' he could paint – and fall in love with. He had a long affair with Elizabeth (Lizzie) Siddal – who caught a cold posing in a bath for Millais's famous painting of the drowned Ophelia – and, after dragging his heels for ten years of their stormy relationship, he married her. Her ill health and laudanum addiction dispatched her not long afterwards. In a grand romantic gesture, he buried unpublished poems with her – only, rather less romantically, to have her remains dug up seven years later, when he wished to publish them after all.

Sudden Light

Rossetti thought that he and Lizzie were fated to be together in this life and the next, and compulsively painted and wrote about her, although he enjoyed diverting interludes with jollier good-time girls.

I have been here before,
But when or how I cannot tell:
I know the grass beyond the door,
The sweet, keen smell,
The sighing sound, the lights around the shore.

You have been mine before,—
How long ago I may not know:
But just when at that swallow's soar
Your neck turned so,
Some veil did fall,— I knew it all of yore.

Has this been thus before?
And shall not thus time's eddying flight
Still with our lives our love restore

In death's despite,
And day and night yield one delight once more?

Emily Dickinson (1830–86)

Dickinson was by all accounts a vivacious girl until something – perhaps an unrequited love in her mid-twenties – caused her to withdraw from the world. A vision in white, she retreated into the house; even the doctor had to diagnose her from a challenging distance and, though she loved children, she sometimes simply dangled treats for them from her windows. Her eccentricities caused her to be known locally as 'the Myth'. Only a handful of poems appeared during her lifetime – publishers didn't appreciate her innovative style – though almost two thousand were discovered after her death, neatly bound, along with fragments scribbled on recipes (she was a keen cook), envelopes and scraps of paper. The first posthumous editions 'corrected' her idiosyncrasies, and it was only in 1955 that Dickinson's poems appeared as she had written them.

Parting

My life closed twice before its close;
It yet remains to see
If Immortality unveil
A third event to me,

So huge, so hopeless to conceive
As these that twice befell.
Parting is all we know of heaven,
And all we need of hell.

Christina Rossetti (1830–94)

Christina was the youngest sister of D. G. **Rossetti**, although as personalities they were the proverbial chalk and cheese. A devout spinster who declined two suitors on religious grounds and worked charitably amongst fallen women, she forswore even the fleshly temptations of chess and the theatre. She modelled for her brother and other Pre-Raphaelite painters, though always for demurely sacred subjects, most notably for Christ in Holman Hunt's *The Light of the World*. The atmospheric carol 'In the Bleak Midwinter' numbers among her poems.

A Birthday

My heart is like a singing bird
Whose nest is in a watered shoot;
My heart is like an apple tree
Whose boughs are bent with thickset fruit;
My heart is like a rainbow shell
That paddles in a halcyon sea;
My heart is gladder than all these
Because my love is come to me.

Raise me a dais of silk and down;
Hang it with vair and purple dyes;
Carve it in doves and pomegranates,
And peacocks with a hundred eyes;
Work it in gold and silver grapes,
In leaves and silver fleurs-de-lys;
Because the birthday of my life
Is come, my love is come to me.

Vair – the fur of a type of red squirrel.

Goblin Market [extracts]

Beautifully illustrated by Christina's brother, *Goblin Market* was presented as a nursery fable, though numerous critics writing in less innocent times have read shades of sauciness into its most succulent passages. Naughty Laura gorges herself on goblin fruit. When she sickens, her goody-goody sister Lizzie redeems her by getting very sticky at the market.

One may lead a horse to water,
Twenty cannot make him drink.
Though the goblins cuffed and caught her,
Coaxed and fought her,
Bullied and besought her,
Scratched her, pinched her black as ink,
Kicked and knocked her,
Mauled and mocked her,
Lizzie uttered not a word;
Would not open lip from lip
Lest they should cram a mouthful in:
But laughed in heart to feel the drip
Of juice that syruped all her face,
And lodged in dimples of her chin,
And streaked her neck which quaked like curd.

. . .

She cried 'Laura,' up the garden,
'Did you miss me?
Come and kiss me.
Never mind my bruises,
Hug me, kiss me, suck my juices
Squeezed from goblin fruits for you,
Goblin pulp and goblin dew.
Eat me, drink me, love me;

Laura, make much of me:
For your sake I have braved the glen
And had to do with goblin merchant men.'

A Short Glossary of Poetic Forms

Ballad – A poem intended for singing, usually with short verses and frequently a chorus. Generally tells a story, often one inspired by folk tales, and hence may have no single author. Like the ballade, it originated in medieval France.

Ballade – A poetic form popular in medieval France, made up of seven-, eight- or ten-line stanzas (usually three of these), with each concluding on the same line as a refrain, and a final four-line stanza, traditionally addressed to a prince. It was revived in English in the nineteenth century by, among others, **Rossetti**, and in the twentieth **Chesterton** was a noted practitioner.

Blank verse – Poetry that has no rhyme scheme, but has a regular metre. Much of Shakespeare's drama is in blank verse, as is **Milton**'s *Paradise Lost*.

Ode – Derived from the Greek for 'song', the ode is a long, serious lyric poem which was developed in Greek drama.

Elegy – The term originally referred to composition in elegiac couplets, where the second line of a couplet is a syllable shorter than the first, but is now generally understood to denote a reflective poem of mourning.

Epigram – Originally a poem inscribed on tombs in ancient Greece, the epigram was used more satirically by the Romans, and the term came to be used for a short poem with a witty ending. It is now also applied to pithy sayings.

Free verse – Verse with no rhyme scheme and variable metre, but which might still have rhythmic elements to distinguish it from prose.

Limerick – A short, usually comic and often rude jingle consisting of five lines, popularized by **Lear**'s *Book of Nonsense.*

Lyric – Originally a Greek song accompanied by a lyre, now applied to short, expressive, emotional poems which were especially popular among Romantic poets (*see* p.44).

Metre – The traditionally regular pattern formed by the syllables of a poem.

Rondeau – A French verse of, strictly, ten, thirteen or fifteen lines, with the first line or lines repeated at the close.

Lewis Carroll (1832–98)

The pioneer of the 'she-woke-up-and-it-was-all-a-dream' trope of storytelling so beloved of schoolchildren, Lewis Carroll was the pen-name of Charles Lutwidge Dodgson, a mild-mannered mathematics lecturer at Oxford University. He entertained ten-year-old Alice Liddell with what would become *Alice's Adventures in Wonderland* at a picnic. Although endless commentaries have sought to pin complex meanings to the *Alice* books, children loved them, and love them still, because they defy the Duchess in proposing no moral whatsoever. Alice is a pragmatic creature who takes all of Wonderland's weirdness in her very Victorian stride.

Jabberwocky

'Twas brillig, and the slithy toves
Did gyre and gimble in the wabe;
All mimsy were the borogoves,
And the mome raths outgrabe.

'Beware the Jabberwock, my son!
The jaws that bite, the claws that catch!
Beware the Jubjub bird, and shun
The frumious Bandersnatch!'

He took his vorpal sword in hand;
Long time the manxome foe he sought –
So rested he by the Tumtum tree,
And stood awhile in thought.

And, as in uffish thought he stood,
The Jabberwock, with eyes of flame,
Came whiffling through the tulgey wood,
And burbled as it came!

One, two! One, two! And through and through
The vorpal blade went snicker-snack!
He left it dead, and with its head
He went galumphing back.

'And hast thou slain the Jabberwock?
Come to my arms, my beamish boy!
O frabjous day! Callooh! Callay!'
He chortled in his joy.

'Twas brillig, and the slithy toves
Did gyre and gimble in the wabe;
All mimsy were the borogoves,
And the mome raths outgrabe.

Thomas Hardy (1840–1928)

Although now better known for his novels, Hardy saw himself as a poet all his life. He initially turned to fiction to support himself, but some of his books attracted moral censure – *Jude the Obscure* was even burnt by a bishop – and he returned to poetry. His first wife, Emma, encouraged his work, and their difficult relationship to some extent inspired him. Despite their unhappiness, after her death he found himself flooded with guilt and too-late love that found moving expression in some of his subsequent poems. His second wife, Florence, previously his assistant, apparently endured this patiently. His body is buried in Poets' Corner at Westminster Abbey, but his heart is either interred alongside his first wife in the churchyard at Stinsford, Dorset, or, more colourfully, was stolen by a naughty cat while awaiting burial.

In Time of 'The Breaking of Nations'

Written in 1915, during the First World War, this gentle poem shows Hardy in an uncharacteristically optimistic mood.

Only a man harrowing clods
In a slow silent walk
With an old horse that stumbles and nods
Half asleep as they stalk.

Only thin smoke without flame
From the heaps of couch-grass;
Yet this will go onward the same
Though Dynasties pass.

Yonder a maid and her wight
Come whispering by:
War's annals will cloud into night
Ere their story die.

Afterwards

When the Present has latched its postern
    behind my tremulous stay,
And the May month flaps its glad green leaves like wings,
Delicate-filmed as new-spun silk, will the neighbours say,
'He was a man who used to notice such things'?

If it be in the dusk when, like an eyelid's soundless blink,
The dewfall-hawk comes crossing the shades to alight
Upon the wind-warped upland thorn, a gazer may think,
'To him this must have been a familiar sight'.

If I pass during some nocturnal blackness, mothy and warm,
When the hedgehog travels furtively over the lawn,
One may say, 'He strove that such innocent
    creatures should come to no harm,
But he could do little for them; and now he is gone'.

If, when hearing that I have been stilled
    at last, they stand at the door,
Watching the full-starred heavens that winter sees,
Will this thought rise on those who will meet my face no more,
'He was one who had an eye for such mysteries'?

And will any say when my bell of quittance
    is heard in the gloom,
And a crossing breeze cuts a pause in its outrollings,
Till they swell again, as they were a new bell's boom,
'He hears it not now, but used to notice such things'?

The Darkling Thrush

I leant upon a coppice gate
When Frost was spectre-gray,

And Winter's dregs made desolate
The weakening eye of day.
The tangled bine-stems scored the sky
Like strings of broken lyres,
And all mankind that haunted nigh
Had sought their household fires.

The land's sharp features seemed to be
The Century's corpse outleant,
His crypt the cloudy canopy,
The wind his death-lament.
The ancient pulse of germ and birth
Was shrunken hard and dry,
And every spirit upon earth
Seemed fervourless as I.

At once a voice arose among
The bleak twigs overhead
In a full-hearted evensong
Of joy illimited;
An aged thrush, frail, gaunt, and small,
In blast-beruffled plume,
Had chosen thus to fling his soul
Upon the growing gloom.

So little cause for carolings
Of such ecstatic sound
Was written on terrestrial things
Afar or nigh around,
That I could think there trembled through
His happy good-night air
Some blessed Hope, whereof he knew
And I was unaware.

Gerard Manley Hopkins (1844–89)

Hopkins felt his poetic vocation at odds with his religious calling as a Jesuit, and resolved not to write unless directed by his Order, as in 'The Wreck of the Deutschland', which commemorates five nuns lost at sea. His distinctive 'sprung rhythm' – peppered with unexpected stresses – was a little too innovative for the Jesuit magazine that declined to publish the poem, and for years after his death his verses circulated only among his friends. His modern style and posthumous publication meant that he was thought of as a twentieth-century poet, though he was undoubtedly a product of his own Victorian age. A small and gloomy man, haunted by his religious doubts and suppressed sexuality, it is cheering to know that he uttered some rather unlikely last words on his deathbed: 'I am so happy, I am so happy.'

Pied Beauty

Glory be to God for dappled things—
For skies of couple-colour as a brinded cow;
For rose-moles all in stipple upon trout that swim;
Fresh-firecoal chestnut-falls, finches' wings;
Landscape plotted and pieced—fold, fallow, and plough;
And áll trádes, their gear and tackle and trim.

All things counter, original, spare, strange;
Whatever is fickle, freckled (who knows how?)
With swift, slow; sweet, sour; adazzle, dim;
He fathers-forth whose beauty is past change:
Praise him.

Emma Lazarus (1849–87)

Born into a wealthy New York Jewish family, Lazarus was politicized by the anti-Jewish pogroms in Russia of 1881–4. She wrote in defence of the Jewish people and assisted in the education of those who had fled anti-Semitism in Europe.

The New Colossus

Lazarus wrote this sonnet to raise funds to build the pedestal for the Statue of Liberty (the statue itself being a gift to the United States from France). It references the Colossus of Rhodes, one of the Seven Wonders of the Ancient World, and the 'twin cities' are New York City and Brooklyn, not yet joined when she composed these lines in 1883.

Not like the brazen giant of Greek fame,
With conquering limbs astride from land to land;
Here at our sea-washed, sunset gates shall stand
A mighty woman with a torch, whose flame
Is the imprisoned lightning, and her name
Mother of Exiles. From her beacon-hand
Glows world-wide welcome; her mild eyes command
The air-bridged harbor that twin cities frame.
'Keep, ancient lands, your storied pomp!' cries she
With silent lips. 'Give me your tired, your poor,
Your huddled masses yearning to breathe free,
The wretched refuse of your teeming shore.
Send these, the homeless, tempest-tost to me,
I lift my lamp beside the golden door!'

W. E. Henley (1849–1903)

As a child, Henley contracted tuberculosis of the bone, which caused him long years of agony and cost him a leg. He spent a year under the care of the pioneering surgeon

Joseph Lister in Edinburgh, where he was introduced to Robert Louis **Stevenson**. Stevenson later admitted that Henley had been the inspiration for *Treasure Island*'s one-legged pirate, Long John Silver. Henley's invalid daughter, Margaret, was the model for J. M. Barrie's Wendy (Barrie invented the name, from Margaret's pronunciation of 'friend' as 'fwend' or 'fwendy'), though she died, aged only six, ten years before *Peter Pan* was first performed, and so, heartbreakingly, never saw or read the play.

Invictus

'Invictus' (Latin: unconquered, invincible) was written after the amputation of Henley's leg, in a staggeringly defiant mood given the circumstances. It has been quoted by, among others, Winston Churchill, Martin Luther King and Nelson Mandela.

Out of the night that covers me,
Black as the Pit from pole to pole,
I thank whatever gods may be
For my unconquerable soul.

In the fell clutch of circumstance
I have not winced nor cried aloud.
Under the bludgeonings of chance
My head is bloody, but unbowed.

Beyond this place of wrath and tears
Looms but the Horror of the shade,
And yet the menace of the years
Finds, and shall find, me unafraid.

It matters not how strait the gate,
How charged with punishments the scroll,
I am the master of my fate;
I am the captain of my soul.

Robert Louis Stevenson (1850–94)

Born in Edinburgh, Stevenson was too sickly to follow the family profession as a lighthouse engineer, and chased a healthy climate for most of his adult life. At Edinburgh University he rejected religion, which grieved his parents, and took to haunting the city's dark underbelly and cultivating bohemian airs, including changing his middle name from Lewis, and wearing velvet coats. The swashbuckling *Treasure Island* was his first novel and brought him fame, though *The Strange Adventures of Dr Jekyll and Mr Hyde* is his dark masterpiece: inspired by a nightmare, it was written and printed in just ten weeks.

Requiem

Stevenson settled in Samoa, where the natives revered him as the local storyteller. He was buried there, overlooking the sea, with this verse inscribed upon his tomb.

Under the wide and starry sky,
Dig the grave and let me lie.
Glad did I live and gladly die,
And I laid me down with a will.

This be the verse you grave for me:
Here he lies where he longed to be;
Home is the sailor, home from sea,
And the hunter home from the hill.

Bed in Summer

In winter I get up at night
And dress by yellow candle-light.
In summer quite the other way,
I have to go to bed by day.

I have to go to bed and see
The birds still hopping on the tree,

Or hear the grown-up people's feet
Still going past me in the street.

And does it not seem hard to you,
When all the sky is clear and blue,
And I should like so much to play,
To have to go to bed by day?

Ella Wheeler Wilcox (1850–1919)

Ella Wheeler was born to Wisconsin farmers and wrote to support her family. Her mildly steamy poems were hugely popular with readers, though critics sniffily included her in some anthologies of 'worst poems'. Both she and her husband were spiritualists (their only child died as a baby), and they promised each other that whoever 'passed over' first would return with messages for the survivor. During the First World War, she believed that her husband instructed her (from beyond the grave) to visit the Allied forces in France, which she duly did. She recited poems to the troops, and lectured them helpfully about venereal disease.

Solitude

'Solitude' was inspired by a weeping widow Wilcox met on the way to a ball: having comforted her all the way there, she found that her own party spirit had evaporated.

Laugh, and the world laughs with you,
Weep, and you weep alone,
For sad old earth must borrow it's mirth,
But has trouble enough of its own.
Sing, and the hills will answer;
Sigh, it is lost on the air,
The echoes bound to a joyful sound,
But shrink from voicing care.

Rejoice, and men will seek you;
Grieve, and they turn and go.
They want full measure of all your pleasure,
But they do not need your woe.
Be glad, and your friends are many,
Be sad, and you lose them all;
There are none to decline your nectared wine,
But alone you must drink life's gall.

Feast, and your halls are crowded,
Fast, and the world goes by.
Succeed and give – and it helps you live,
But no man can help you die;
There is room in the halls of pleasure
For a large and lordly train,
But one by one we must all file on
Through the narrow aisles of pain.

Oscar Wilde (1854–1900)

The flamboyant, Irish-born Wilde was celebrated for his biting wit as well as for his brilliant plays. It was his complicated private life, however, that made him infamous. Though married, he visited rent boys and formed a relationship with Lord Alfred Douglas, ('Bosie'), which outraged the boy's father, the Marquess of Queensberry. Queensberry, who clearly hadn't consulted a dictionary first, presented the now famous playwright with a card addressed 'For Oscar Wilde posing Somdomite'. Wilde sued Queensberry for libel, thus setting in motion a train of events that eventually saw him sentenced to two years' imprisonment in Reading Gaol. He left England for good on his release. He spent his last years in cheap Parisian hotels, and his tomb, on which pilgrims lavish lipstick kisses, can be seen in that city's Père Lachaise cemetery.

The Ballad of Reading Gaol [extract]

I never saw a man who looked
With such a wistful eye
Upon that little tent of blue
Which prisoners call the sky,
And at every drifting cloud that went
With sails of silver by.

. . .

I only knew what hunted thought
Quickened his step, and why
He looked upon the garish day
With such a wistful eye;
The man had killed the thing he loved,
And so he had to die.

. . .

Yet each man kills the thing he loves,
By each let this be heard,
Some do it with a bitter look,
Some with a flattering word.
The coward does it with a kiss,
The brave man with a sword!

Some kill their love when they are young,
And some when they are old;
Some strangle with the hands of Lust,
Some with the hands of Gold:
The kindest use a knife, because
The dead so soon grow cold.

Some love too little, some too long,
Some sell, and others buy;
Some do the deed with many tears,
And some without a sigh:
For each man kills the thing he loves,
Yet each man does not die.

He does not die a death of shame
On a day of dark disgrace,
Nor have a noose about his neck,
Nor a cloth upon his face,
Nor drop feet foremost through the floor
Into an empty space.

A. E. Housman (1859–1936)

Despite his brilliance, Alfred Edward Housman failed his degree at Oxford, possibly because he had become desperately attached to a fellow undergraduate though he suppressed his sexuality for most of his life – perhaps Wilde's fate was a cautionary tale. He worked in the Patent Office for over a decade, publishing whenever he could, but became a Professor of Latin at University College, London and, later, at Cambridge. Since teaching Latin was his day job he was reluctant to make money out of his poetry, returning royalty cheques to his publisher (who must have thought him a dream author) until 1926.

Loveliest of Trees, the Cherry Now

Loveliest of trees, the cherry now
Is hung with bloom along the bough,
And stands about the woodland ride
Wearing white for Eastertide.

Now, of my threescore years and ten,
Twenty will not come again,
And take from seventy springs a score,
It only leaves me fifty more.

And since to look at things in bloom
Fifty springs are little room,
About the woodlands I will go
To see the cherry hung with snow.

Sir Henry Newbolt (1862–1938)

Newbolt was a model Victorian: a school head boy who grew up extolling the virtues of patriotism and team spirit, and was terribly active on all sorts of benevolent committees. 'Drake's Drum', his rousing poem about the mythical percussion instrument that will summon Sir Francis Drake to England's aid in her darkest hour, has been drummed (sorry) into many generations of schoolboys.

Vitaï Lampada

The poem refers to Newbolt's old school, Clifton College in Bristol. It was used as propaganda during the First World War, invoking a spirit of hearty English fair play.

There's a breathless hush in the Close to-night –
Ten to make and the match to win –
A bumping pitch and a blinding light,
An hour to play and the last man in.
And it's not for the sake of a ribboned coat,
Or the selfish hope of a season's fame,
But his Captain's hand on his shoulder smote –
'Play up! play up! and play the game!'

The sand of the desert is sodden red, –
Red with the wreck of a square that broke; –

The Gatling's jammed and the colonel dead,
And the regiment blind with dust and smoke.
The river of death has brimmed his banks,
And England's far, and Honour a name,
But the voice of a schoolboy rallies the ranks:
'Play up! play up! and play the game!'

This is the word that year by year,
While in her place the School is set,
Every one of her sons must hear,
And none that hears it dare forget.
This they all with a joyful mind
Bear through life like a torch in flame,
And falling fling to the host behind –
'Play up! play up! and play the game!'

Vitaï Lampada – Latin: 'the torch of life'; *square* – four-sided combat formation into which an infantry battalion would retire if attacked in the open; *Gatling* – an early form of hand-operated machine gun.

Rudyard Kipling (1865–1936)

Kipling is so associated with India that Leonard Woolf (Virginia's husband) wondered whether his depictions of Anglo-Indian life were really so accurate, or whether life imitated Kipling. His poems, stories and novels – including *The Jungle Book* – were hugely successful, but his identification with imperial jingoism diminished his post-war popularity. He declined both the Laureateship and a knighthood, but became the first British winner of the Nobel Prize in Literature in 1907, and remains its youngest recipient. His old age was somewhat melancholy after his only son, John, was killed in 1915. Kipling felt profoundly guilty – he had used his influence to get John a commission (his eyesight would otherwise have excluded him from service). John's body was never found.

If—

This was voted the nation's favourite poem in a 1995 BBC survey, and was inspired by the disastrous 'Jameson Raid' that contributed to the outbreak of the second Boer War in 1899.

If you can keep your head when all about you
Are losing theirs and blaming it on you,
If you can trust yourself when all men doubt you,
But make allowance for their doubting too;
If you can wait and not be tired by waiting,
Or being lied about, don't deal in lies,
Or being hated, don't give way to hating,
And yet don't look too good, nor talk too wise:

If you can dream – and not make dreams your master;
If you can think – and not make thoughts your aim;
If you can meet with Triumph and Disaster
And treat those two impostors just the same;
If you can bear to hear the truth you've spoken
Twisted by knaves to make a trap for fools,
Or watch the things you gave your life to, broken,
And stoop and build 'em up with worn-out tools:

If you can make one heap of all your winnings
And risk it on one turn of pitch-and-toss,
And lose, and start again at your beginnings
And never breathe a word about your loss;
If you can force your heart and nerve and sinew
To serve your turn long after they are gone,
And so hold on when there is nothing in you
Except the Will which says to them: 'Hold on!'

If you can talk with crowds and keep your virtue,

Or walk with Kings – nor lose the common touch,
If neither foes nor loving friends can hurt you,
If all men count with you, but none too much;
If you can fill the unforgiving minute
With sixty seconds' worth of distance run,
Yours is the Earth and everything that's in it,
And – which is more – you'll be a Man, my son!

A Smuggler's Song

If you wake at midnight, and hear a horse's feet,
Don't go drawing back the blind, or looking in the street.
Them that asks no questions isn't told a lie.
Watch the wall, my darling, while the Gentlemen go by!

Five and twenty ponies,
Trotting through the dark –
Brandy for the Parson,
'Baccy for the Clerk;
Laces for a lady, letters for a spy,
And watch the wall, my darling, while the Gentlemen go by!

Running round the woodlump if you chance to find
Little barrels, roped and tarred, all full of brandy-wine,
Don't you shout to come and look, nor use 'em for your play.
Put the brishwood back again – and they'll be gone next day!

If you see the stable-door setting open wide;
If you see a tired horse lying down inside;
If your mother mends a coat cut about and tore;
If the lining's wet and warm – don't you ask no more!

If you meet King George's men, dressed in blue and red,
You be careful what you say, and mindful what is said.

If they call you 'pretty maid', and chuck you 'neath the chin,
Don't you tell where no one is, nor yet where no one's been!

Knocks and footsteps round the house – whistles after dark –
You've no call for running out till the house-dogs bark.
Trusty's here, and Pincher's here, and see how dumb they lie –
They don't fret to follow when the Gentlemen go by!

If you do as you've been told, 'likely there's a chance,
You'll be give a dainty doll, all the way from France,
With a cap of Valenciennes, and a velvet hood –
A present from the Gentlemen, along o' being good!

Five and twenty ponies,
Trotting through the dark –
Brandy for the Parson,
'Baccy for the Clerk;
Them that asks no questions isn't told a lie -
Watch the wall, my darling, while the Gentlemen go by!

Valenciennes – a type of lace, named after the French town where it was made.

Tommy [extracts]

'Tommy' is the generic name for a British soldier, and comes from 'Thomas Atkins', a name used as a specimen on official army forms.

I went into a public-'ouse to get a pint o' beer,
The publican 'e up an' sez, 'We serve no red-coats here.'
The girls be'ind the bar they laughed an' giggled fit to die,
I outs into the street again an' to myself sez I:
O it's Tommy this, an' Tommy that, an' 'Tommy, go away';
But it's 'Thank you, Mister Atkins', when
    the band begins to play,

The band begins to play, my boys, the band begins to play,
O it's 'Thank you, Mister Atkins', when the band begins to play.

. . .

Yes, makin' mock o' uniforms that guard you while you sleep
Is cheaper than them uniforms, an' they're starvation cheap;
An' hustlin' drunken soldiers when they're goin' large a bit
Is five times better business than paradin' in full kit.
Then it's Tommy this, an' Tommy that,
    an' 'Tommy, 'ow's yer soul?'
But it's 'Thin red line of 'eroes' when the drums begin to roll,
The drums begin to roll, my boys, the drums begin to roll,
O it's 'Thin red line of 'eroes' when the drums begin to roll.

. . .

You talk o' better food for us, an' schools, an' fires, an' all:
We'll wait for extry rations if you treat us rational.
Don't mess about the cook-room slops, but prove it to our face
The Widow's Uniform is not the soldier-man's disgrace.
For it's Tommy this, an' Tommy that, an'
    'Chuck him out, the brute!'
But it's 'Saviour of 'is country' when the guns begin to shoot;
An' it's Tommy this, an' Tommy that, an' anything you please;
An' Tommy ain't a bloomin' fool – you bet that Tommy sees!

Widow's Uniform – the queen's uniform, 'the Widow' being a reference to Queen Victoria.

W. B. Yeats (1865–1939)

Born in Dublin, William Butler Yeats was fascinated by Irish folk culture, and by mysticism and the occult. An Irish nationalist, he entertained a hopeless passion for the fiery Republican heiress Maud Gonne, to whom he dedicated his early poems. He proposed to her without success many times, and later even tried his luck with her daughter, equally unsuccessfully. In 1917, having proposed fruitlessly to three women in a year, he married his much younger wife Georgie at the age of fifty-two, after meeting her at a séance. He founded, and wrote for, Dublin's Abbey Theatre and was active as a journalist and politician, becoming a senator of the Irish Free State when it was established. He was awarded the Nobel Prize in Literature in 1923, the first Irish writer to receive it. Yeats died and was buried in France, but in 1948 his body was exhumed and reburied in Co. Sligo, where he had spent much of his childhood.

Sailing to Byzantium

That is no country for old men. The young
In one another's arms, birds in the trees
– Those dying generations – at their song,
The salmon-falls, the mackerel-crowded seas,
Fish, flesh, or fowl, commend all summer long
Whatever is begotten, born, and dies.
Caught in that sensual music all neglect
Monuments of unageing intellect.

An aged man is but a paltry thing,
A tattered coat upon a stick, unless
Soul clap its hands and sing, and louder sing
For every tatter in its mortal dress,
Nor is there singing school but studying
Monuments of its own magnificence;
And therefore I have sailed the seas and come
To the holy city of Byzantium.

O sages standing in God's holy fire
As in the gold mosaic of a wall,
Come from the holy fire, perne in a gyre,
And be the singing-masters of my soul.
Consume my heart away; sick with desire
And fastened to a dying animal
It knows not what it is; and gather me
Into the artifice of eternity.

Once out of nature I shall never take
My bodily form from any natural thing
But such a form as Grecian goldsmiths make
Of hammered gold and gold enamelling
To keep a drowsy Emperor awake;
Or set upon a golden bough to sing
To lords and ladies of Byzantium
Of what is past, or passing, or to come.

The Lake Isle of Innisfree

I will arise and go now, and go to Innisfree,
And a small cabin build there, of clay and wattles made:
Nine bean-rows will I have there, a hive for the honey-bee,
And live alone in the bee-loud glade.

And I shall have some peace there, for
    peace comes dropping slow,
Dropping from the veils of the morning
    to where the cricket sings;
There midnight's all a glimmer, and noon a purple glow,
And evening full of the linnet's wings.

I will arise and go now, for always night and day
I hear lake water lapping with low sounds by the shore;

While I stand on the roadway, or on the pavements grey,
I hear it in the deep heart's core.

Aedh Wishes for the Cloths of Heaven

Aedh is a character from Celtic myth. Later collections usually replace 'Aedh' in the title with 'He'.

Had I the heavens' embroidered cloths,
Enwrought with golden and silver light,
The blue and the dim and the dark cloths
Of night and light and the half light,
I would spread the cloths under your feet:
But I, being poor, have only my dreams;
I have spread my dreams under your feet;
Tread softly because you tread on my dreams.

Hilaire Belloc (1870–1953)

The half-French Belloc was brought up in England and educated at Oxford, where he earned the nickname 'Old Thunder' for winning a debate that he suddenly joined from the floor of the chamber. H. G. Wells later said that 'debating Mr Belloc is like arguing with a hailstorm.' He had hoped for a fellowship at All Souls', and believed that he had been rejected because of his ardent Catholicism – something the interviewers could hardly have missed, as he placed a statue of the Virgin Mary on the desk during his examination. His *Cautionary Tales for Children* (1907) have delighted, educated and terrified generations of children. During the First World War he worked as a propagandist, confiding to his dear friend G. K. **Chesterton** that 'it is sometimes necessary to lie damnably in the interests of the nation.' The two writers were so close that George Bernard Shaw referred to them as the singular 'Chesterbelloc'.

Tarantella

The tarantella is a fast, whirling Italian folk dance which was thought to be a cure for
a tarantula's bite, in which case it might be danced for days.

Do you remember an Inn, Miranda?
Do you remember an Inn?
And the tedding and the spreading
Of the straw for a bedding,
And the fleas that tease in the High Pyrenees,
And the wine that tasted of the tar?
And the cheers and the jeers of the young muleteers
(Under the vine of the dark verandah)?
Do you remember an Inn, Miranda,
Do you remember an Inn?
And the cheers and the jeers of the young muleteeers
Who hadn't got a penny,
And who weren't paying any,
And the hammer at the doors and the Din?
And the Hip! Hop! Hap!
Of the clap
Of the hands to the twirl and the swirl
Of the girl gone chancing,
Glancing,
Dancing,
Backing and advancing,
Snapping of a clapper to the spin
Out and in –
And the Ting, Tong, Tang, of the Guitar!
Do you remember an Inn,
Miranda?
Do you remember an Inn!

Never more;
Miranda,
Never more.
Only the high peaks hoar:
And Aragon a torrent at the door.
No sound
In the walls of the Halls where falls

The tread
Of the feet of the dead to the ground
No sound:
But the boom
Of the far Waterfall like Doom.

First World War Poetry

The 'Great War' of 1914–18 encouraged thousands to put pen to paper, and plays and novels appeared as well as poetry. Ordinary people turned to writing to process their experiences, and a generation of 'trench poets' sprang up almost overnight. In 1916 a canny London publisher printed an anthology called *Soldier Poets: Songs of the Fighting Men* – with a lightweight edition for the boys in the trenches – and a second volume followed in 1918. It rapidly became important to the reading public whether the poets had seen military action, and aside from collections and anthologies, poems – of very varying quality – were printed in newspapers and magazines throughout the war. **Brooke**'s patriotic war poetry and tragic death set the tone, and his *1914 and Other Poems* became a runaway bestseller, while the disenchanted work of poets like **Sassoon** and **Owen**, among others, found few takers at the time.

After the Armistice in November 1918 most of the war poets stopped writing – nobody wanted to mention the war – and only Brooke continued to sell, bringing comfort to the grieving nation. However, at the end of the 1920s the 'War Books Controversy' was ignited when memoirs of the trenches, including Robert Graves's *Goodbye to All That* and Erich Maria Remarque's *All Quiet on the Western Front*, began to appear, and ate away at any remaining romantic illusions about the conflict. Now the balance has tipped heavily in favour of writers whose patriotism turned to horrified disgust in the face of the horrors of the Western Front.

Laurence Binyon (1869–1943)

Both before and after the First World War Binyon worked among the British Museum's collections of drawings and prints. He was appointed Norton Professor of Poetry at Harvard in 1933. Ezra Pound was a close friend of his and gave him the slightly undignified nickname 'BinBin'.

For the Fallen

Binyon was too old to enlist when the First World War broke out, and wrote this poem in Cornwall in 1914. He had not then visited the Western Front, though he later served there as a Red Cross orderly. The poem is now read during Remembrance Day services around the world, especially the fourth verse, and adorns numerous memorials to the fallen of 'the war that will end all wars'.

With proud thanksgiving, a mother for her children,
England mourns for her dead across the sea.
Flesh of her flesh they were, spirit of her spirit,
Fallen in the cause of the free.

Solemn the drums thrill: Death august and royal
Sings sorrow up into immortal spheres.

There is music in the midst of desolation
And a glory that shines upon our tears.

They went with songs to the battle, they were young,
Straight of limb, true of eye, steady and aglow.
They were staunch to the end against odds uncounted,
They fell with their faces to the foe.

They shall grow not old, as we that are left grow old:
Age shall not weary them, nor the years condemn.
At the going down of the sun and in the morning
We will remember them.

They mingle not with their laughing comrades again;
They sit no more at familiar tables of home;
They have no lot in our labour of the day-time;
They sleep beyond England's foam.

But where our desires are and our hopes profound,
Felt as well-spring that is hidden from sight,
To the innermost heart of their own land they are known
As the stars are known to the Night;

As the stars that shall be bright when we are dust,
Moving in marches upon the heavenly plain,
As the stars that are starry in the time of our darkness,
To the end, to the end they remain.

W. H. Davies (1871–1940)

The title of William Henry Davies's 1908 *Autobiography of a Super-Tramp* gives an unsubtle clue to his lifestyle. Raised in Newport, South Wales, he spent some years on the road in the United States and Canada, losing a leg train-hopping. On his return he continued to live rough in London, keeping his poetry a secret from the other vagrants. Davies printed his first poems at his own expense and sold the volume by posting copies to names he found in *Who's Who*; perhaps to his surprise, they proved fairly popular. In 1923 he married a streetwalker many years his junior, whom he picked up on the Edgware Road, and wrote about their courtship in the lightly fictionalized *Young Emma*, which was published after her death in 1980.

Leisure

What is this life if, full of care,
We have no time to stand and stare?—

No time to stand beneath the boughs,
And stare as long as sheep or cows:

No time to see, when woods we pass,
Where squirrels hide their nuts in grass:

No time to see, in broad daylight,
Streams full of stars, like skies at night:

No time to turn at Beauty's glance,
And watch her feet, how they can dance:

No time to wait till her mouth can
Enrich that smile her eyes began?

A poor life this if, full of care,
We have no time to stand and stare.

John McCrae (1872–1918)

McCrae, a leading Canadian doctor, enlisted in 1914. A year later while he was running a field hospital at Ypres, his twenty-two-year-old friend Alexis Helmer was killed and, the chaplain being absent, McCrae officiated at his funeral. This inspired his most famous poem, though accounts of its composition differ: some have him scribbling it in twenty minutes after the ceremony, and others describe him writing it the next day, sitting on the steps of an ambulance overlooking the makeshift grave. Legend has it that he rejected the poem, but a fellow soldier rescued the discarded page and submitted it for publication. McCrae died in France in 1918, of pneumonia.

In Flanders Fields

This poem inspired an answering verse by R. W. Lillard: ' ... Fear not that you have died for naught, / The torch ye threw to us we caught ... ' Today it is often read at Remembrance Day services.

In Flanders fields the poppies blow
Between the crosses, row on row,
That mark our place; and in the sky
The larks, still bravely singing, fly
Scarce heard amid the guns below.

We are the Dead. Short days ago
We lived, felt dawn, saw sunset glow,
Loved and were loved, and now we lie
In Flanders fields.

Take up our quarrel with the foe:
To you from failing hands we throw
The torch; be yours to hold it high.
If ye break faith with us who die
We shall not sleep, though poppies grow
In Flanders fields.

Walter de la Mare (1873–1956)

Until he was in his mid-thirties, de la Mare fitted his writing around his somewhat prosaic day job at Standard Oil. He produced novels, as well as poetry and reviews, and the popular anthology for children, *Come Hither*. Throughout his life he stubbornly ignored all changing fashions to write on his cherished themes of childhood and fantasy, and he was a master at creating a truly creepy atmosphere, as his most famous poem shows.

The Listeners

'The Listeners' appeared in 1912, a date that renders Thomas **Hardy**'s appraisal of it as the finest poem of the century a little less impressive as a compliment.

'Is there anybody there?' said the Traveller,
Knocking on the moonlit door;
And his horse in the silence champed the grasses
Of the forest's ferny floor:
And a bird flew up out of the turret,
Above the Traveller's head:
And he smote upon the door again a second time;
'Is there anybody there?' he said.
But no one descended to the Traveller;
No head from the leaf-fringed sill
Leaned over and looked into his grey eyes,
Where he stood perplexed and still.
But only a host of phantom listeners
That dwelt in the lone house then
Stood listening in the quiet of the moonlight
To that voice from the world of men:
Stood thronging the faint moonbeams on the dark stair,
That goes down to the empty hall,
Hearkening in an air stirred and shaken

By the lonely Traveller's call.
And he felt in his heart their strangeness,
Their stillness answering his cry,
While his horse moved, cropping the dark turf,
'Neath the starred and leafy sky;
For he suddenly smote on the door, even
Louder, and lifted his head:–
'Tell them I came, and no one answered,
That I kept my word,' he said.
Never the least stir made the listeners,
Though every word he spake
Fell echoing through the shadowiness of the still house
From the one man left awake:
Ay, they heard his foot upon the stirrup,
And the sound of iron on stone,
And how the silence surged softly backward,
When the plunging hoofs were gone.

Silver

Slowly, silently, now the moon
Walks the night in her silver shoon;
This way, and that, she peers, and sees
Silver fruit upon silver trees;
One by one the casements catch
Her beams beneath the silvery thatch;
Couched in his kennel, like a log,
With paws of silver sleeps the dog;
From their shadowy cote the white breasts peep
Of doves in a silver-feathered sleep;
A harvest mouse goes scampering by,
With silver claws, and silver eye;

And moveless fish in the water gleam,
By silver reeds in a silver stream.

G. K. Chesterton (1874–1936)

Despite being rather a scatterbrain, Chesterton managed to produce journalism, biographies, short stories – including the Father Brown mysteries – and the peculiar, anarchic thriller *The Man Who Was Thursday: A Nightmare*. Considerable credit must go to his wife, Frances, who occasionally redirected him by telegram when he had misjudged public transport and arrived at the wrong town. Always a Christian, Chesterton eventually converted to Catholicism, perhaps due to the influence of his bosom friend, Hilaire **Belloc**. Chesterton enjoyed good-natured debates with peers including George Bernard Shaw, and was happy to lampoon his own bear-like figure. He told the stringy Shaw, 'To look at you anyone would think there was a famine in England,' to which Shaw retorted: 'To look at you, anyone would think you caused it.'

The Donkey

When fishes flew and forests walked
And figs grew upon thorn,
Some moment when the moon was blood
Then surely I was born;

With monstrous head and sickening cry
And ears like errant wings,
The devil's walking parody
On all four-footed things.

The tattered outlaw of the earth,
Of ancient crooked will;
Starve, scourge, deride me: I am dumb,
I keep my secret still.

Fools! For I also had my hour;
One far fierce hour and sweet:
There was a shout about my ears,
And palms before my feet.

Robert Frost (1874–1963)

Frost was dogged by poor health and bereavements: his father died young leaving his mother with just $8, only two of his six children outlived him, his wife predeceased him by twenty-five years, and mental illness haunted the family. Despite these setbacks, Frost achieved huge popularity, winning the Pulitzer Prize four times and declaiming at John F. Kennedy's inauguration as President in 1961, aged eighty-six. He had written a new poem for the occasion but, with the sun half blinding him, found he couldn't read it, and so recited his 1942 poem 'The Gift Outright' from memory, to rapturous applause. A shy man, he was initially horrified by fame but lectured to pay the bills, and he developed a winning folksy style that brought him many fans. Frost retired to his New Hampshire farm and is buried in Vermont, his gravestone proclaiming that he had fought a 'lover's quarrel with the world'.

The Road Not Taken

Two roads diverged in a yellow wood,
And sorry I could not travel both
And be one traveller, long I stood
And looked down one as far as I could
To where it bent in the undergrowth;

Then took the other, as just as fair,
And having perhaps the better claim,
Because it was grassy and wanted wear;
Though as for that, the passing there
Had worn them really about the same,

And both that morning equally lay
In leaves no step had trodden black.
Oh, I kept the first for another day!
Yet knowing how way leads on to way,
I doubted if I should ever come back.

I shall be telling this with a sigh
Somewhere ages and ages hence:
Two roads diverged in a wood, and I –
I took the one less travelled by,
And that has made all the difference.

Stopping By Woods on a Snowy Evening

Frost stayed up writing all one midwinter night in 1922. He stepped out into the snow-gilded morning and wrote this poem in minutes, likening it to a hallucination.

Whose woods these are I think I know.
His house is in the village, though;
He will not see me stopping here
To watch his woods fill up with snow.

My little horse must think it queer
To stop without a farmhouse near
Between the woods and frozen lake
The darkest evening of the year.

He gives his harness bells a shake
To ask if there is some mistake.
The only other sound's the sweep
Of easy wind and downy flake.

The woods are lovely, dark, and deep,
But I have promises to keep,

And miles to go before I sleep,
And miles to go before I sleep.

Edward Thomas (1878–1917)

Born in London, Edward Thomas moved to the country and worked as a full-time writer to support a growing family. He was encouraged to take up poetry by Robert **Frost**, and much of his verse is a clear-eyed evocation of the English countryside. He is one of the finest of the Great War poets – remarkably, given that his poems almost never mention his experiences at the front, where he was killed in the Battle of Arras.

Adlestrop

Adlestrop is a small village in Gloucestershire, and the poem records a train journey Thomas made in June 1914, a few weeks before war broke out. The line was closed in 1966, and the station is now a private house.

Yes. I remember Adlestrop—
The name, because one afternoon
Of heat the express-train drew up there
Unwontedly. It was late June.

The steam hissed. Someone cleared his throat.
No one left and no one came
On the bare platform. What I saw
Was Adlestrop—only the name

And willows, willow-herb, and grass,
And meadowsweet, and haycocks dry,
No whit less still and lonely fair
Than the high cloudlets in the sky.

And for that minute a blackbird sang

Close by, and round him, mistier,
Farther and farther, all the birds
Of Oxfordshire and Gloucestershire

John Masefield (1878–1967)

At seventeen Masefield took the unorthodox step of running away *from* sea and,
like **Davies**, lived rough in America for a time. He developed a love for sailors'
salty stories and, on his return to England, began writing poems, essays, plays and
novels, among them the much-loved children's novel *The Box of Delights*. Masefield
was old enough not to have to enlist during the First World War but, like his
friend **Binyon**, he went to the Western Front as a medical orderly, and later wrote
Gallipoli in response to German propaganda. In 1930 he became a hard-working
and humble Laureate. His longevity in the post was second only to Tennyson's, and
he always submitted his poems to *The Times* with a stamped addressed envelope,
in case they were rejected.

Cargoes

Quinquireme of Nineveh from distant Ophir
Rowing home to haven in sunny Palestine,
With a cargo of ivory,
And apes and peacocks,
Sandalwood, cedarwood, and sweet white wine.

Stately Spanish galleon coming from the Isthmus,
Dipping through the Tropics by the palm-green shores,
With a cargo of diamonds,
Emeralds, amethysts,
Topazes, and cinnamon, and gold moidores.

Dirty British coaster with a salt-caked smoke stack
Butting through the Channel in the mad March days,

With a cargo of Tyne coal,
Road-rail, pig-lead,
Firewood, iron-ware, and cheap tin trays.

Quinquireme – galley with five banks of oars; *Ophir* – though mentioned several times in the Old Testament, this ancient port remains unidentified; *moidore* – Portuguese gold piece also used in England.

Sea-Fever

Pedants, please note that the first line is often misquoted as 'I must *go* down to the seas again', as it scanned better when set to music. Fans of sci-fi trivia (no less numerous, I'm sure) might like to know that the 'tall ship' is referenced in *Star Trek V*.

I must down to the seas again, to the lonely sea and the sky,
And all I ask is a tall ship and a star to steer her by,
And the wheel's kick and the wind's song
    and the white sail's shaking,
And a grey mist on the sea's face and a grey dawn breaking.

I must down to the seas again, for the call of the running tide
Is a wild call and a clear call that may not be denied;
And all I ask is a windy day with the white clouds flying,
And the flung spray and the blown spume,
    and the sea-gulls crying.

I must down to the seas again, to the vagrant gypsy life,
To the gull's way and the whale's way where
    the wind's like a whetted knife;
And all I ask is a merry yarn from a laughing fellow-rover,
And quiet sleep and a sweet dream when the long trick's over.

Alfred Noyes (1880–1958)

Noyes is almost certainly the finest poet produced by Wolverhampton (to date). During the First World War he worked on propaganda in a department of the Ministry of Information headed by John Buchan, author of *The Thirty-Nine Steps*. Though at university Noyes won more praise for his rowing than his studies, he later taught English Literature at Princeton and was fiercely anti-Modernist, reserving particular scorn for James Joyce. In later years he lost his sight, but continued to dictate his works.

The Highwayman [extract]

Trussed to a loaded musket by the soldiers waiting to capture her outlaw lover, Bess manages to shoot herself to warn him of the trap. Unfortunately this grand gesture proves futile, for the highwayman returns in fury and the long arm of the law catches up with him in the end, the soldiers shooting him down 'like a dog on the highway'.

The wind was a torrent of darkness among the gusty trees,
The moon was a ghostly galleon tossed upon cloudy seas,
The road was a ribbon of moonlight over the purple moor,
And the highwayman came riding –
Riding – riding –
The highwayman came riding, up to the old inn-door.

He'd a French cocked-hat on his forehead,
    a bunch of lace at his chin,
A coat of the claret velvet, and breeches of brown doe-skin;
They fitted with never a wrinkle: his
    boots were up to the thigh!
And he rode with a jewelled twinkle,
His pistol butts a-twinkle,
His rapier hilt a-twinkle, under the jewelled sky.

Over the cobbles he clattered and clashed in the dark inn-yard,
And he tapped with his whip on the shutters,
    but all was locked and barred;
He whistled a tune to the window, and
    who should be waiting there
But the landlord's black-eyed daughter,
Bess, the landlord's daughter,
Plaiting a dark red love-knot into her long black hair.

And dark in the dark old inn-yard a stable-wicket creaked
Where Tim the ostler listened; his face was white and peaked;
His eyes were hollows of madness, his hair like mouldy hay,
But he loved the landlord's daughter,
The landlord's red-lipped daughter;
Dumb as a dog he listened, and he heard the robber say –

'One kiss, my bonny sweetheart, I'm after a prize to-night,
But I shall be back with the yellow gold
    before the morning light;
Yet, if they press me sharply, and harry me through the day,
Then look for me by moonlight,
Watch for me by moonlight,
I'll come to thee by moonlight, though Hell should bar the way.'
. . .

D. H. Lawrence (1885–1930)

David Herbert Lawrence grew up in a less than tranquil household, where his boorish father, a coal miner, clashed frequently with his mother, a teacher with suffocating aspirations for her cherished son. Lawrence's novels include the infamous *Lady Chatterley's Lover* (not published in the UK until 1960, after a famously unsuccessful prosecution for obscenity). His novels were too experimental and too risqué for readers and the authorities at the time and he was largely unappreciated. In 1914 he ran away with Frieda Weekley, the wife of a professor, who abandoned her family for him. Their relationship was turbulent; once, during a row at dinner, Lawrence stabbed a fork into Frieda's hand. During the First World War – to which Lawrence was vocally opposed, despite being too ill to fight – they were driven out of Cornwall because the locals feared they might be German spies. Ironically when the couple moved to Frieda's hometown of Metz, Lawrence was arrested on suspicion of being an English spy, which did nothing to soothe his persecution complex.

Snake [extracts]

A snake came to my water-trough
On a hot, hot day, and I in pyjamas for the heat,
To drink there.

In the deep, strange-scented shade of the great dark carob-tree
I came down the steps with my pitcher
And must wait, must stand and wait, for there
    he was at the trough before me.

He reached down from a fissure in the earth-wall in the gloom
And trailed his yellow-brown slackness soft-bellied
    down, over the edge of the stone trough
And rested his throat upon the stone bottom,
And where the water had dripped from
    the tap, in a small clearness,

He sipped with his straight mouth,
Softly drank through his straight gums, into his slack long body,
Silently.

Someone was before me at my water-trough,
And I, like a second comer, waiting.

He lifted his head from his drinking, as cattle do,
And looked at me vaguely, as drinking cattle do,
And flickered his two-forked tongue from
    his lips, and mused a moment,
And stooped and drank a little more,
Being earth-brown, earth-golden from the
    burning bowels of the earth
On the day of Sicilian July, with Etna smoking.

The voice of my education said to me
He must be killed,
For in Sicily the black, black snakes are
    innocent, the gold are venomous.

And voices in me said, If you were a man
You would take a stick and break him now, and finish him off.

But must I confess how I liked him,
How glad I was he had come like a guest in
    quiet, to drink at my water-trough
And depart peaceful, pacified, and thankless,
Into the burning bowels of this earth?

. . .

I looked round, I put down my pitcher,
I picked up a clumsy log
And threw it at the water-trough with a clatter.

I think it did not hit him,
But suddenly that part of him that was left
    behind convulsed in undignified haste,
Writhed like lightning, and was gone
Into the black hole, the earth-lipped fissure in the wall-front,
At which, in the intense still noon, I stared with fascination.

And immediately I regretted it.
I thought how paltry, how vulgar, what a mean act!
I despised myself and the voices of my
    accursed human education.

And I thought of the albatross,
And I wished he would come back, my snake.

For he seemed to me again like a king,
Like a king in exile, uncrowned in the underworld,
Now due to be crowned again.

And so, I missed my chance with one of the lords
Of life.
And I have something to expiate;
A pettiness.

Siegfried Sassoon (1886–1967)

Sassoon grew up as a wealthy country gent, before the First World War changed everything. He joined up with alacrity on the first day of the war, and won both the Military Cross and the nickname 'Mad Jack' for his bravery on the Western Front. In 1917 he was sent back to Britain to recover from a wound and, desperately shaken by what he had witnessed in the trenches, made a courageous public statement that the war was being dragged out unnecessarily by the top brass. The authorities promptly diagnosed him with 'shell shock' and sent him to a military hospital in Scotland to recover his wits. There he met Wilfred **Owen**, to whom he became a friend and mentor: his notes survive on an early draft of the latter's 'Anthem for Doomed Youth' (p.155). He returned to the front line but was wounded again, this time badly enough to take no further part in the fighting. His war poems attacked the squalor and senselessness of trench warfare, the generation of generals lining up Britain's young men as cannon fodder, and those back home cosily dosing themselves up on Rupert **Brooke**'s misty-eyed patriotism. Perhaps predictably, they weren't to the public's taste at the time, and appeared in only a handful of the many wartime anthologies.

The General

This poem reflects the age-old conflict between 'teeth' and 'tail' – that is, between the fighting men at the front and the staff officers and other non-combatants to the rear.

'Good-morning; good-morning!' the General said
When we met him last week on our way to the line.
Now the soldiers he smiled at are most of 'em dead,
And we're cursing his staff for incompetent swine.
'He's a cheery old card,' grunted Harry to Jack
As they slogged up to Arras with rifle and pack.

But he did for them both by his plan of attack.

Everyone Sang

Sassoon was recuperating on 11 November 1918 when the Armistice ended the war on the Western Front. He wrote this a few months later, in April 1919. In his autobiographical *Goodbye To All That* Robert Graves tells us that 'everyone' celebrating the Armistice did not include him; at the time, he found himself 'cursing and sobbing and thinking of the dead'.

Everyone suddenly burst out singing;
And I was filled with such delight
As prisoned birds must find in freedom,
Winging wildly across the white
Orchards and dark-green fields; on; on; and out of sight.

Everyone's voice was suddenly lifted,
And beauty came like the setting sun.
My heart was shaken with tears; and horror
Drifted away . . . O but every one
Was a bird; and the song was wordless;
    the singing will never be done.

Rupert Brooke (1887–1915)

Brooke was a six-foot dreamboat, called 'the most handsome young man in England' by W. B. **Yeats**, and apparently irresistible to both women and men. His charisma, charm and intelligence (and those good looks) endeared him to creative and influential friends, including E. M. Forster, Bernard Shaw and the Bloomsbury set. He is most famous for his war poems, which glow with the patriotic idealism of the Great War's early years, before **Sassoon**, **Owen** and others exposed the horrors of trench warfare. He did, of course, die abroad, but it was in fact from an infected mosquito bite en route to Gallipoli in 1915.

The Soldier

The combination of his early death and this poem made Brooke a hero despite his relative lack of combat experience. It was praised by Churchill and even used as a recruitment aid. Poor Brooke's grave is on the Greek island of Skyros, where his comrades had to bury him without much ceremony under a stone cairn, although a more elegant marker was put up later.

If I should die, think only this of me:
That there's some corner of a foreign field
That is forever England. There shall be
In that rich earth a richer dust concealed;
A dust whom England bore, shaped, made aware,
Gave, once, her flowers to love, her ways to roam,
A body of England's, breathing English air,
Washed by the rivers, blest by suns of home.

And think, this heart, all evil shed away,
A pulse in the Eternal mind, no less
Gives somewhere back the thoughts by England given,
Her sights and sounds; dreams happy as her day;
And laughter, learnt of friends; and gentleness,
In hearts at peace, under an English heaven.

The Old Vicarage, Grantchester [extract]

Written in Berlin while Brooke recovered from yet another disastrous love affair, this poem evokes an idyllic, rural England that had probably already vanished at the time of writing in 1912. I risk disturbing your enjoyment of the scene by revealing that the vicarage's current occupants are Lord (Jeffrey) and Lady (Mary) Archer . . .

Ah God! to see the branches stir
Across the moon at Grantchester!
To smell the thrilling-sweet and rotten

Unforgettable, unforgotten
River-smell, and hear the breeze
Sobbing in the little trees.
Say, do the elm-clumps greatly stand
Still guardians of that holy land?
The chestnuts shade, in reverend dream,
The yet unacademic stream?
Is dawn a secret shy and cold
Anadyomene, silver-gold?
And sunset still a golden sea
From Haslingfield to Madingley?
And after, ere the night is born,
Do hares come out about the corn?
Oh, is the water sweet and cool,
Gentle and brown, above the pool?
And laughs the immortal river still
Under the mill, under the mill?
Say, is there Beauty yet to find?
And Certainty? and Quiet kind?
Deep meadows yet, for to forget
The lies, and truths, and pain? . . . oh! yet
Stands the Church clock at ten to three?
And is there honey still for tea?

The Georgian Poets

Georgian poetry centres around a bestselling series of anthologies planned by **Brooke**, Harold Monro and Edward Marsh. Five volumes were published between 1912 and 1922, and they brought together younger poets aiming for a simpler style that moved away from what they saw as pompous Victorian sentiment. Poets such as **Lawrence**, **Masefield**, **de la Mare**, **Housman** and **Graves** were included, and the early collections injected a new freshness into English poetry. However, the declining quality of the work, the fact that some of the poets, including Graves, objected to the label, and the scorn of modernizers such as **Eliot** and Ezra Pound – who felt that a post-Great War world needed new poetry – saw Georgian poetry fall from favour, though many of its proponents are still esteemed by critics and enjoyed by readers.

T. S. Eliot (1888–1965)

Thomas Stearns Eliot was born in Missouri, but in 1914 he settled in England, and married Vivien Haigh-Wood, who would participate in the writing of some of his poems, including *The Waste Land*. After they separated in 1933, she had a habit of turning up to his lectures holding a placard proclaiming 'I am the wife he abandoned'. Vivien was later committed to a mental hospital, where she died in 1947. Eliot went on to marry Valerie Fletcher, his secretary at the London publishing house Faber and Faber, where he supported many up-and-coming poets. In 1927 he became a British subject, and also joined the Church of England. His staggeringly wide range of references and literary in-jokes have led some critics to accuse him of being wilfully difficult or obscure. For his part, Eliot felt that the reader should have to work a little to enjoy poetry, although he did allow that the experience should be pleasurable from the first reading.

The Love Song of J. Alfred Prufrock [extract]

It is well worth seeking out the full text of this poem, which Eliot completed at the astonishingly young age of twenty-three.

Let us go then, you and I,
When the evening is spread out against the sky
Like a patient etherized upon a table;
Let us go, through certain half-deserted streets,
The muttering retreats
Of restless nights in one-night cheap hotels
And sawdust restaurants with oyster-shells:
Streets that follow like a tedious argument
Of insidious intent
To lead you to an overwhelming question . . .
Oh, do not ask, 'What is it?'
Let us go and make our visit.

In the room the women come and go
Talking of Michelangelo.

The yellow fog that rubs its back upon the window-panes,
The yellow smoke that rubs its muzzle on the window-panes,
Licked its tongue into the corners of the evening,
Lingered upon the pools that stand in drains,
Let fall upon its back the soot that falls from chimneys,
Slipped by the terrace, made a sudden leap,
And seeing that it was a soft October night,
Curled once about the house, and fell asleep.

The Waste Land [extract]

A long poem in five parts, *The Waste Land* draws on fertility legends, Christian symbolism, the poet's own biography and countless other sources – as well as its author's copious scholarly, if eccentric, footnotes – to examine the world in the years after the First World War.

I The Burial of the Dead

April is the cruellest month, breeding
Lilacs out of the dead land, mixing
Memory and desire, stirring
Dull roots with spring rain.
Winter kept us warm, covering
Earth in forgetful snow, feeding
A little life with dried tubers.

Summer surprised us, coming over the Starnbergersee
With a shower of rain; we stopped in the colonnade,
And went on in sunlight, into the Hofgarten,
And drank coffee, and talked for an hour.
Bin gar keine Russin, stamm' aus Litauen, echt deutsch.
And when we were children, staying at the arch-duke's,
My cousin's, he took me out on a sled,
And I was frightened. He said, Marie,
Marie, hold on tight. And down we went.
In the mountains, there you feel free.
I read, much of the night, and go south in the winter.

What are the roots that clutch, what branches grow
Out of this stony rubbish? Son of man,
You cannot say, or guess, for you know only
A heap of broken images, where the sun beats,
And the dead tree gives no shelter, the cricket no relief,

And the dry stone no sound of water. Only
There is shadow under this red rock,
(Come in under the shadow of this red rock),
And I will show you something different from either
Your shadow at morning striding behind you
Or your shadow at evening rising to meet you;
I will show you fear in a handful of dust.

Macavity – The Mystery Cat [extract]

Macavity is one of the most disreputable characters in Eliot's *Old Possum's Book of Practical Cats*, which inspired the musical *Cats*.

Macavity's a Mystery Cat: he's called the Hidden Paw –
For he's the master criminal who can defy the Law.
He's the bafflement of Scotland Yard,
    the Flying Squad's despair:
For when they reach the scene of crime – *Macavity's not there!*

Macavity, Macavity, there's no one like Macavity,
He's broken every human law, he breaks the law of gravity.
His powers of levitation would make a fakir stare,
And when you reach the scene of crime – *Macavity's not there!*
You may seek him in the basement, you may look up in the air –
But I tell you once and once again, *Macavity's not there!*

Macavity's a ginger cat, he's very tall and thin;
You would know him if you saw him, for his eyes are sunken in.
His brow is deeply lined with thought,
    his head is highly domed;
His coat is dusty from neglect, his whiskers are uncombed.
He sways his head from side to side, with
    movements like a snake;
And when you think he's half asleep, he's always wide awake.

Macavity, Macavity, there's no one like Macavity,
For he's a fiend in feline shape, a monster of depravity.
You may meet him in a by-street, you
    may see him in the square –
But when a crime's discovered, then *Macavity's not there!*

He's outwardly respectable. (They say he cheats at cards.)
And his footprints are not found in any file of Scotland Yard's.
And when the larder's looted, or the jewel-case is rifled,
Or when the milk is missing, or another Peke's been stifled,
Or the greenhouse glass is broken, and the trellis past repair –
Ay, there's the wonder of the thing! *Macavity's not there!*

Wilfred Owen (1893–1918)

Owen enlisted in 1915, but he was invalided with stress to hospital in Scotland in 1917, where he was befriended by **Sassoon**. Both men felt it their duty to close the vast gap of understanding between the troops at the Front and those left behind. Owen even carried a photograph of casualties with him as a gruesome visual aid. He was awarded the Military Cross, but was killed just a week before the Armistice. Like Sassoon, Owen was undervalued during the war because the folks back home yearned for poets to tell them what they wanted to hear: that the war was just, death in battle glorious, and victory certain. He saw only five of his poems published before his death and was excluded by **Yeats** – who criticized the myth-making his short life attracted – from *The Oxford Book of Modern Verse* in 1936. Gradually, though, he has become the most famous of the Great War poets.

Dulce et Decorum Est

'The old lie', taken from a Latin ode by the first-century BC Roman poet Horace, translates as: 'It is sweet and fitting to die for your country.'

Bent double, like old beggars under sacks,
Knock-kneed, coughing like hags, we cursed through sludge,

Till on the haunting flares we turned our backs
And towards our distant rest began to trudge.
Men marched asleep. Many had lost their boots
But limped on, blood-shod. All went lame; all blind;
Drunk with fatigue; deaf even to the hoots
Of tired, outstripped Five-Nines that dropped behind.

Gas! GAS! Quick, boys! – An ecstasy of fumbling,
Fitting the clumsy helmets just in time;
But someone still was yelling out and stumbling,
And flound'ring like a man in fire or lime . . .
Dim, through the misty panes and thick green light,
As under a green sea, I saw him drowning.

In all my dreams, before my helpless sight,
He plunges at me, guttering, choking, drowning.

If in some smothering dreams you too could pace
Behind the wagon that we flung him in,
And watch the white eyes writhing in his face,
His hanging face, like a devil's sick of sin;
If you could hear, at every jolt, the blood
Come gargling from the froth-corrupted lungs,
Obscene as cancer, bitter as the cud
Of vile, incurable sores on innocent tongues, –
My friend, you would not tell with such high zest
To children ardent for some desperate glory,
The old Lie: Dulce et decorum est
Pro patria mori.

Five-Nines – shells fired from an artillery piece with a calibre of 5.9-inches; *helmets* –
not the familiar steel shrapnel helmet, but a gas helmet, a kind of primitive gas mask
usually consisting of a cloth hood with transparent eyepieces.

Anthem for Doomed Youth

What passing–bells for these who die as cattle?
Only the monstrous anger of the guns.
Only the stuttering rifles' rapid rattle
Can patter out their hasty orisons.
No mockeries for them from prayers or bells,
Nor any voice of mourning save the choirs, –
The shrill, demented choirs of wailing shells;
And bugles calling for them from sad shires.

What candles may be held to speed them all?
Not in the hands of boys, but in their eyes
Shall shine the holy glimmers of good-byes.
The pallor of girls' brows shall be their pall;
Their flowers the tenderness of silent minds,
And each slow dusk a drawing-down of blinds.

Dorothy Parker (1893–1967)

Wisecracking Mrs Parker grew up in New York and wrote for, among others, *Vogue* and *Vanity Fair*. She became the queen bee of the Algonquin Hotel Round Table, a coterie of wits who met each day for lunch in the hotel on West 44th Street to bitch, drink, gossip and generally congratulate themselves. It was a reprehensible new world – women were smoking, drinking, carrying on with men and even, Heaven forbid, dancing the Charleston – but Parker's cool verse often tots up the bitter costs of these freedoms. She had a finely tuned sense of irony, so she no doubt realized – but didn't care – what terribly bad manners it was to die from a heart attack in her seventies, after having written so much about the attractions of suicide.

Résumé

Razors pain you;
Rivers are damp;

Acids stain you;
And drugs cause cramp.
Guns aren't lawful;
Nooses give;
Gas smells awful;
You might as well live.

Unfortunate Coincidence

By the time you swear you're his,
Shivering and sighing,
And he vows his passion is
Infinite, undying –
Lady, make a note of this:
One of you is lying.

FIVE
'Not waving, but drowning'

Stevie Smith (1902–71)

Florence Margaret Smith was nicknamed 'Stevie' after the jockey Steve Donoghue because she was so small. She was mainly brought up by a beloved aunt (whom she called 'Lion'), with whom she lived all her life, never marrying. She produced three novels of thinly veiled autobiography, which caused her a certain amount of grief when people – including George Orwell, with whom she may have had a love affair – thought they recognized themselves. She illustrated her poetry with her own eccentric doodles. Smith focused increasingly on death, though frequently in a rather jaunty tone, and was fascinated by religion. Her readings, in public and for the BBC, won her many fans, including Sylvia **Plath**; sadly, Plath committed suicide before they could meet.

Not Waving but Drowning

Nobody heard him, the dead man,
But still he lay moaning:
I was much further out than you thought
And not waving but drowning.

Poor chap, he always loved larking
And now he's dead
It must have been too cold for him his heart gave way,
They said.

Oh, no no no, it was too cold always
(Still the dead one lay moaning)
I was much too far out all my life
And not waving but drowning.

John Betjeman (1906–84)

Betjeman threw himself into undergraduate life at Oxford with a vengeance – the friendships and carousing, though, rather than the academic side of things. He had brought his teddy bear, Archibald Ormsby-Gore, along for the ride, thereby providing inspiration for his fellow undergraduate, Evelyn Waugh, whose character Sebastian Flyte in *Brideshead Revisited* dotes on a teddy bear named Aloysius. Betjeman later worked as a freelance journalist and broadcaster, publishing his first volume of poetry in 1931. During the Second World War he worked in the British Embassy in Dublin, where the IRA considered assassinating him as a spy, something only revealed many years later. Betjeman was knighted in 1969, and was a popular choice for Poet Laureate in 1972 – he personally replied by hand to every member of the public who sent him a poem.

Slough

Come, friendly bombs, and fall on Slough
It isn't fit for humans now,
There isn't grass to graze a cow
Swarm over, Death!

Come, bombs, and blow to smithereens
Those air-conditioned, bright canteens,
Tinned fruit, tinned meat, tinned milk, tinned beans,
Tinned minds, tinned breath.

Mess up the mess they call a town –
A house for ninety-seven down
And once a week a half-a-crown
For twenty years,

And get that man with double chin
Who'll always cheat and always win,

Who washes his repulsive skin
In women's tears,

And smash his desk of polished oak
And smash his hands so used to stroke
And stop his boring dirty joke
And make him yell.

But spare the bald young clerks who add
The profits of the stinking cad;
It's not their fault that they are mad,
They've tasted Hell.

It's not their fault they do not know
The birdsong from the radio,
It's not their fault they often go
To Maidenhead

And talk of sport and makes of cars
In various bogus Tudor bars
And daren't look up and see the stars
But belch instead.

In labour-saving homes, with care
Their wives frizz out peroxide hair
And dry it in synthetic air
And paint their nails.

Come, friendly bombs, and fall on Slough
To get it ready for the plough.
The cabbages are coming now;
The earth exhales.

A Subaltern's Love Song

There really was a Miss Joan Hunter Dunn. She was twenty-five in 1940 and working in London when Betjeman first saw her and, despite being married, immediately fell for her, although he never declared himself.

Miss J. Hunter Dunn, Miss J. Hunter Dunn,
Furnish'd and burnish'd by Aldershot sun,
What strenuous singles we played after tea,
We in the tournament – you against me!

Love-thirty, love-forty, oh! weakness of joy,
The speed of a swallow, the grace of a boy,
With carefullest carelessness, gaily you won.
I am weak from your loveliness, Joan Hunter Dunn.

Miss Joan Hunter Dunn, Miss Joan Hunter Dunn,
How mad I am, sad I am, glad that you won.
The warm-handled racket is back in its press,
But my shock-headed victor, she loves me no less.

Her father's euonymus shines as we walk,
And swing past the summer-house, buried in talk,
And cool the verandah that welcomes us in
To the six-o'clock news and a lime-juice and gin.

The scent of the conifers, sound of the bath,
The view from my bedroom of moss-dappled path,
As I struggle with double-end evening tie,
For we dance at the Golf Club, my victor and I.

On the floor of her bedroom lie blazer and shorts
And the cream-coloured walls are be-trophied with sports,
And westering, questioning settles the sun
On your low-leaded window, Miss Joan Hunter Dunn.

The Hillman is waiting, the light's in the hall,
The pictures of Egypt are bright on the wall,
My sweet, I am standing beside the oak stair
And there on the landing's the light on your hair.

By roads 'not adopted', by woodlanded ways,
She drove to the club in the late summer haze,
Into nine-o'clock Camberley, heavy with bells
And mushroomy, pine-woody, evergreen smells.

Miss Joan Hunter Dunn, Miss Joan Hunter Dunn,
I can hear from the car park the dance has begun.
Oh! full Surrey twilight! importunate band!
Oh! strongly adorable tennis-girl's hand!

Around us are Rovers and Austins afar,
Above us, the intimate roof of the car,
And here on my right is the girl of my choice,
With the tilt of her nose and the chime of her voice,

And the scent of her wrap, and the words never said,
And the ominous, ominous dancing ahead.
We sat in the car-park till twenty to one
And now I'm engaged to Miss Joan Hunter Dunn.

Louis MacNeice (1907–63)

MacNeice grew up in Belfast, where his father was a fiery Anglican rector. At Oxford he met Auden and Stephen Spender; his first volume of poetry was published while he was still an undergraduate. He took a post in the hard-working and hard-drinking environment of the BBC – Dylan Thomas was a colleague, so the Christmas party must have been raucous – but he managed to produce writing including acclaimed radio drama, as well as poetry. He died unexpectedly, having contracted pneumonia while recording sound effects in a dank cave.

Prayer Before Birth

I am not yet born; O hear me.
Let not the bloodsucking bat or the rat or the stoat
    or the club-footed ghoul come near me.

I am not yet born, console me.
I fear that the human race may with tall walls wall me,
    with strong drugs dope me, with wise lies lure me,
    on black racks rack me, in blood-baths roll me.

I am not yet born; provide me
With water to dandle me, grass to grow for me, trees
    to talk to me, sky to sing to me, birds and a white
    light in the back of my mind to guide me.

I am not yet born; forgive me
For the sins that in me the world shall commit, my
    words when they speak me, my thoughts when
    they think me, my treason engendered by traitors
    beyond me, my life when they murder by means
    of my hands, my death when they live me.

I am not yet born; rehearse me
In the parts I must play and the cues I must take when

old men lecture me, bureaucrats hector me, mountains
frown at me, lovers laugh at me, the white waves call
me to folly and the desert calls me to doom and the
beggar refuses my gift and my children curse me.

I am not yet born; O hear me,
Let not the man who is beast or who thinks
   he is God come near me.

I am not yet born; O fill me
With strength against those who would freeze my humanity,
   would dragoon me into a lethal automaton, would make
   me a cog in a machine, a thing with one face, a thing, and
   against all those who would dissipate my entirety, would
   blow me like thistledown hither and thither or hither and
   thither like water held in the hands would spill me.

Let them not make me a stone and let them not spill me.
Otherwise kill me.

W. H. Auden (1907–73)

Wystan Hugh Auden established a poetic reputation while still an undergraduate at Oxford. T. S. **Eliot** at Faber and Faber published his first book, *Poems*, in 1930, and he was cast as the leader of the 'Oxford Movement' that also included Cecil Day-Lewis, Louis **MacNeice** and Stephen Spender. The turbulence of the 1930s in Europe pitched the young poets, including Auden, towards the political left; he went to Spain as a volunteer on the Republican side in the Spanish Civil War, but left after only a few weeks, appalled. Nine months before the Second World War broke out, he went to live in America, and became a US citizen in 1946. Hugely prolific and experimental, his rejection of Romanticism – he dismissed the poets he called 'Kelly and Sheets' – was vastly influential. He won the Pulitzer Prize for Poetry and was Professor of Poetry at Oxford for five years from 1956. In 1935 he married Erika Mann (daughter of the novelist Thomas Mann), securing her a British passport to escape the Third Reich, but his long-term lover was his friend and collaborator Chester Kallman, an American writer and librettist.

Night Mail

This is the Night Mail crossing the Border,
Bringing the cheque and the postal order,

Letters for the rich, letters for the poor,
The shop at the corner, the girl next door.

Pulling up Beattock, a steady climb:
The gradient's against her, but she's on time.

Past cotton-grass and moorland boulder,
Shovelling white steam over her shoulder,

Snorting noisily, she passes
Silent miles of wind-bent grasses.

Birds turn their heads as she approaches,
Stare from the bushes at her blank-faced coaches.

Sheep-dogs cannot turn her course;
They slumber on with paws across.

In the farm she passes no one wakes,
But a jug in the bedroom gently shakes.

Dawn freshens. Her climb is done.
Down towards Glasgow she descends,
Towards the steam tugs yelping down a glade of cranes,
Towards the fields of apparatus, the furnaces
Set on the dark plain like gigantic chessmen.
All Scotland waits for her:

In dark glens, beside pale-green lochs,
Men long for news.

Letters of thanks, letters from banks,
Letters of joy from girl and boy,
Receipted bills and invitations
To inspect new stock or to visit relations,
And applications for situations,
And timid lovers' declarations,
And gossip, gossip from all the nations,
News circumstantial, news financial,
Letters with holiday snaps to enlarge in,
Letters with faces scrawled on the margin,
Letters from uncles, cousins and aunts,
Letters to Scotland from the South of France,
Letters of condolence to Highlands and Lowlands,
Written on paper of every hue,
The pink, the violet, the white and the blue,
The chatty, the catty, the boring, the adoring,
The cold and official and the heart's outpouring,
Clever, stupid, short and long,
The typed and the printed and the spelt all wrong.

Thousands are still asleep,
Dreaming of terrifying monsters
Or a friendly tea beside the band in Cranston's or Crawford's:
Asleep in working Glasgow, asleep in well-set Edinburgh,
Asleep in granite Aberdeen,
They continue their dreams,
But shall wake soon and hope for letters,
And none will hear the postman's knock
Without a quickening of the heart.
For who can bear to feel himself forgotten?

Funeral Blues

This poem was made famous by John Hannah's dulcet Scottish tones in the 1994 film *Four Weddings and a Funeral*.

Stop all the clocks, cut off the telephone,
Prevent the dog from barking with a juicy bone,
Silence the pianos and with muffled drum
Bring out the coffin, let the mourners come.

Let aeroplanes circle moaning overhead
Scribbling on the sky the message He is Dead,
Put crêpe bows round the white necks of the public doves,
Let the traffic policemen wear black cotton gloves.

He was my North, my South, my East and West,
My working week and my Sunday rest,
My noon, my midnight, my talk, my song;
I thought that love would last for ever: I was wrong.

The stars are not wanted now: put out every one;
Pack up the moon and dismantle the sun;
Pour away the ocean and sweep up the wood;
For nothing now can ever come to any good.

John Pudney (1909–77)

After leaving school aged sixteen, Pudney worked briefly as an estate agent before embarking on a writing career, composing most of his poems during the Second World War. His copious output included one of the first 'toilet books', a history of the noble loo called *The Smallest Room: A Discreet Survey Through the Ages*. He is also said to have been the first person to utter a taboo wood on the BBC, when he read his poem 'Combat Report' during a wartime radio broadcast; the poem's last line is: "'He burnt out in the air; that's how the poor sod died.'"

For Johnny

During the Second World War Pudney served as an intelligence officer in the RAF, and he wrote this lament for lost pilots on the back of an envelope during an enemy air raid.

Do not despair
For Johnny-head-in-air;
He sleeps as sound
As Johnny underground.

Fetch out no shroud
For Johnny-in-the-cloud;
And keep your tears
For him in after years.

Better by far
For Johnny-the-bright-star,
To keep your head,
And see his children fed.

Dylan Thomas (1914–53)

The mercurial Welsh poet who knew no Welsh, Thomas was the son of a Swansea teacher. His poems would number more than ninety-nine if he hadn't had a day-job working for the BBC and a serious drink habit that led to his early death. Besides his poetry, he wrote a successful radio play, *Under Milk Wood*, as well as a collection of autobiographical stories entitled, in a satirical nod to James Joyce, *Portrait of the Artist as a Young Dog*. In 1937, against his parents' wishes, Thomas married a dancer, Caitlin MacNamara – whom, appropriately enough, he had met in a pub – though their relationship was always tempestuous. He was known for pilfering items from hosts' houses to pay for booze – and, according to Kingsley Amis, peeing on their sofas – but Caitlin also drank. He won passionate fans with his bombastic readings – though his one television appearance has sadly been lost.

Do Not Go Gentle Into That Good Night

This poem was written in response to his father's final illness.

Do not go gentle into that good night,
Old age should burn and rave at close of day;
Rage, rage against the dying of the light.

Though wise men at their end know dark is right,
Because their words had forked no lightning they
Do not go gentle into that good night.

Good men, the last wave by, crying how bright
Their frail deeds might have danced in a green bay,
Rage, rage against the dying of the light.

Wild men who caught and sang the sun in flight,
And learn, too late, they grieved it on its way,
Do not go gentle into that good night.

Grave men, near death, who see with blinding sight
Blind eyes could blaze like meteors and be gay,
Rage, rage against the dying of the light.

And you, my father, there on the sad height,
Curse, bless, me now with your fierce tears, I pray.
Do not go gentle into that good night.
Rage, rage against the dying of the light.

Philip Larkin (1922–85)

Larkin claimed that although he didn't choose poetry, poetry chose him. A reluctant career librarian, he spent most of his working life at the University of Hull cultivating his grumpy, hermit-like image, although in fact he had several long-term relationships. Larkin's down-to-earth tone – and the naughty words, probably – made him the best-loved poet in the country in his later years, though, typically, he declined the Laureateship, preferring to maintain his status as the perpetual outsider looking gloomily in. The publication of his *Selected Letters* in 1992 and of Andrew Motion's official biography a year later revealed a more unsavoury side – including a taste for pornography and some pretty unpalatable, notably racist, views – but the popularity of his poems endures.

This Be The Verse

A jolly parody of this poem states instead: 'They tuck you up, your mum and dad. / They may not mean to but they do. / They give you all the quilts they have / And add some pillows just for you.'

They fuck you up, your mum and dad.
They may not mean to, but they do.
They fill you with the faults they had
And add some extra, just for you.

But they were fucked up in their turn
By fools in old-style hats and coats,
Who half the time were soppy-stern
And half at one another's throats.

Man hands on misery to man.
It deepens like a coastal shelf.
Get out as early as you can,
And don't have any kids yourself.

Toads

Why should I let the toad *work*
Squat on my life?
Can't I use my wit as a pitchfork
And drive the brute off?

Six days of the week it soils
With its sickening poison –
Just for paying a few bills!
That's out of proportion.

Lots of folk live on their wits:
Lecturers, lispers,
Losels, loblolly-men, louts –
They don't end as paupers;

Lots of folk live up lanes
With fires in a bucket,
Eat windfalls and tinned sardines –
They seem to like it.

Their nippers have got bare feet,
Their unspeakable wives

Are skinny as whippets – and yet
No one actually *starves*.

Ah, were I courageous enough
To shout *Stuff your pension!*
But I know, all too well, that's the stuff
That dreams are made on:

For something sufficiently toad-like
Squats in me, too;
Its hunkers are heavy as hard luck,
And cold as snow,

And will never allow me to blarney
My way of getting
The fame and the girl and the money
All at one sitting.

I don't say, one bodies the other
One's spiritual truth;
But I do say it's hard to lose either,
When you have both.

Sylvia Plath (1932–63)

Precocious from the beginning, Plath drove herself ruthlessly both at Smith College and during a prestigious internship at *Mademoiselle* magazine in New York in 1953, and suffered a breakdown. The six months she spent recovering in a private clinic inspired her novel *The Bell Jar*. Plath moved to England to study at Cambridge in 1955. She bit Ted Hughes on the face when he kissed her at a party, and they were married within months. When she discovered his affair with the exotic thrice-married Assia Wevill the marriage collapsed. A distraught Plath plunged herself into a creative frenzy, rising at dawn to write the furious poems for which she is best remembered. In February 1963, during the bitterest English winter of the century, she gassed herself in the oven. Her first volume of poetry had been published in 1960, and *Ariel*, the collection that cemented her extraordinary reputation, appeared two years after her death.

Daddy [extracts]

It's probably unnecessary, in the light of this poem, to state that Plath had a complex relationship with her German father, Otto, who died when she was a child. Here, as in many of her poems, his image mingles with that of Hughes.

You do not do, you do not do
Any more, black shoe
In which I have lived like a foot
For thirty years, poor and white,
Barely daring to breathe or Achoo.

Daddy, I have had to kill you.
You died before I had time–
Marble-heavy, a bag full of God,
Ghastly statue with one gray toe
Big as a Frisco seal

And a head in the freakish Atlantic

Where it pours bean green over blue
In the waters off beautiful Nauset.
I used to pray to recover you.
Ach, du.
. . .

Not God but a swastika
So black no sky could squeak through.
Every woman adores a Fascist,
The boot in the face, the brute
Brute heart of a brute like you.

You stand at the blackboard, daddy,
In the picture I have of you,
A cleft in your chin instead of your foot
But no less a devil for that, no not
Any less the black man who

Bit my pretty red heart in two.
I was ten when they buried you.
At twenty I tried to die
And get back, back, back to you.
I thought even the bones would do.

But they pulled me out of the sack,
And they stuck me together with glue.
And then I knew what to do.
I made a model of you,
A man in black with a Meinkampf look

And a love of the rack and the screw.
And I said I do, I do.
So daddy, I'm finally through.

The black telephone's off at the root,
The voices just can't worm through.

If I've killed one man, I've killed two –
The vampire who said he was you
And drank my blood for a year,
Seven years, if you want to know.
Daddy, you can lie back now.

There's a stake in your fat black heart
And the villagers never liked you.
They are dancing and stamping on you.
They always *knew* it was you.
Daddy, daddy, you bastard, I'm through.

Jenny Joseph (1932–)

Born in Birmingham, Jenny Joseph studied at St Hilda's College, Oxford and has
worked as a journalist, lecturer and pub landlady. She has written in various genres
including poetry, fiction, children's books, and even a gardening book, *Led by the
Nose: A Garden of Smells* (2002). Her story in prose and verse, *Persephone,* won the
1986 James Tait Black Memorial Prize for Fiction.

Warning

When I am an old woman I shall wear purple
With a red hat which doesn't go, and doesn't suit me.
And I shall spend my pension on brandy and summer gloves
And satin sandals, and say we've no money for butter.
I shall sit down on the pavement when I'm tired
And gobble up samples in shops and press alarm bells
And run my stick along the public railings
And make up for the sobriety of my youth.

I shall go out in my slippers in the rain
And pick flowers in other people's gardens
And learn to spit.

You can wear terrible shirts and grow more fat
And eat three pounds of sausages at a go
Or only eat bread and pickle for a week
And hoard pens and pencils and beermats and things in boxes.

But now we must have clothes that keep us dry
And pay our rent and not swear in the street
And set a good example for the children.
We must have friends to dinner and read the papers.

But maybe I ought to practise a little now?
So people who know me are not too shocked and surprised
When suddenly I am old, and start to wear purple.

Seamus Heaney (1939–)

Heaney was born into a Catholic farming family in County Derry, Northern Ireland, close to the border with the Republic. In his later work, he addressed the Troubles in Ireland and also wrote about Iron Age corpses discovered in peat bogs. The image of the poor old bog people, apparently sacrificed to a greedy god and preserved in the memory-bank of the earth, inspired some of the poems in his collection *North* (1975). Heaney's prestigious appointments have included Professor of Rhetoric and Oratory at Harvard and Professor of Poetry at Oxford. He won the Nobel Prize in Literature in 1995, and in 1999 his admired *Beowulf: A New Translation* beat *Harry Potter and the Prisoner of Azkaban* to the Whitbread Book of the Year Award. His public readings are vastly popular: the audiences have even been called 'Heaneyboppers'.

Digging

Between my finger and my thumb
The squat pen rests; snug as a gun.

Under my window a clean rasping sound
When the spade sinks into gravelly ground:
My father, digging. I look down

Till his straining rump among the flowerbeds
Bends low, comes up twenty years away
Stooping in rhythm through potato drills
Where he was digging.

The coarse boot nestled on the lug, the shaft
Against the inside knee was levered firmly.
He rooted out tall tops, buried the bright edge deep
To scatter new potatoes that we picked
Loving their cool hardness in our hands.

By God, the old man could handle a spade,
Just like his old man.

My grandfather cut more turf in a day
Than any other man on Toner's bog.
Once I carried him milk in a bottle
Corked sloppily with paper. He straightened up
To drink it, then fell to right away
Nicking and slicing neatly, heaving sods
Over his shoulder, going down and down
For the good turf. Digging.

The cold smell of potato mold, the squelch and slap
Of soggy peat, the curt cuts of an edge

Through living roots awaken in my head.
But I've no spade to follow men like them.

Between my finger and my thumb
The squat pen rests.
I'll dig with it.

Wendy Cope (1945–)

Wendy Cope produces pitch-perfect parodies in a wide variety of genres, with echoes of Larkin and Betjeman. Educated at Oxford's St Hilda's College, she taught in primary schools before becoming a columnist for *The Spectator* in 1986. She created the persona of the banal bard of Tulse Hill, Jason Strugnell, in her bestselling 1986 volume of poems, *Making Cocoa for Kingsley Amis*. Her poetry has attracted critical acclaim and awards as well as a wide readership, and she has also edited anthologies and written verses for children.

Bloody Men

Bloody men are like bloody buses –
You wait for about a year
And as soon as one approaches your stop
Two or three others appear.

You look at them flashing their indicators
Offering you a ride.
You're trying to read the destinations,
You haven't much time to decide.

If you make a mistake, there is no turning back.
Jump off, and you'll stand there and gaze
While the cars, the taxis and the lorries go by
And the minutes, the hours, the days.

Carol Ann Duffy (1955–)

In 2009 Duffy became the first female, and the first openly gay, Laureate, succeeding Andrew Motion. She intends to donate the annual fee to fund a new poetry prize, but wisely asked for the butt of sherry (nominally, about 108 gallons) to be delivered upfront when she was told that the previous incumbent was still waiting for his. Her work has attracted many awards, including the Whitbread (now the Costa) in 1993 and the T. S. Eliot Prize in 2005. When one of her poems was excised from a school syllabus in case it promoted knife crime, she responded with the poem 'Mrs Schofield's GCSE', which points out, quite rightly, that Shakespeare is positively dripping in gore.

Valentine

Not a red rose or a satin heart.

I give you an onion.
It is a moon wrapped in brown paper.
It promises light
like the careful undressing of love.

Here.
It will blind you with tears
like a lover.
It will make your reflection
a wobbling photo of grief.

I am trying to be truthful.

Not a cute card or a kissogram.

I give you an onion.
Its fierce kiss will stay on your lips,
possessive and faithful
as we are,
for as long as we are.

Take it.
Its platinum loops shrink to a wedding-ring,
if you like.
Lethal.
Its scent will cling to your fingers,
cling to your knife.

SELECT BIBLIOGRAPHY

A Poet's Guide to Britain (BBC 1 May 2009) [TV broadcast]

Abrams, M. H. (ed.), *Norton Anthology of English Literature,* Volume 1 (WW Norton, 1993)

Abrams, M.H., et al. (eds), *Norton Anthology of English Literature,* Volume II (WW Norton, 1993)

Ackroyd, Peter, *Albion: The Origins of the English Imagination* (Chatto & Windus, 2002)

Andronik, Catherine M., *Wildly Romantic: The English Romantic Poets: The Mad, The Bad and the Dangerous* (Henry Holt, 2007)

Answers.com [website] <www.answers.com>

Classic Encyclopedia [website] <www.1911encyclopedia.org>

Creighton, T.R.N. (ed.), *Poems of Thomas Hardy, A New Selection* (Macmillan, 1974)

Donoghue, Denis, *Yeats* (Fontana, 1971)

Drabble, Margaret (ed.), *The Oxford Companion to English Literature* (Oxford University Press, sixth edition, 2000, revised 2006)

Ferguson, Margaret, Salter, Mary Jo and Stallworthy, Jon (eds), *The Norton Anthology of Poetry* (W. W. Norton, fifth edition, 2005)

Gill, Brendan, Introduction to *The Collected Dorothy Parker* (Penguin Classics, 2001)

Graves, Robert, *Good-Bye to All That* (Jonathan Cape, 1929)

Gross, John (ed.), *The New Oxford Book of Literary Anecdotes* (Oxford University Press, 2006)

Gurr, Elizabeth and de Piro, Celia (eds), *Nineteenth and Twentieth Century Women Poets* (Oxford University Press, 1997)

Hall, Donald (ed.), *The Oxford Book of American Literary Anecdotes* (Oxford University Press, 1981)

Hamilton, Ian (ed.) *The Oxford Companion to Twentieth-Century Poetry in English* (Oxford University Press, 1994)

Hawksley, Lucinda, *Lizzie Siddal: The Tragedy of a Pre-Raphaelite Supermodel* (Andre Deutsch, 2004)

Hayward, John (ed.), *Robert Herrick: Selected Poems* (Penguin, 1961)

Holmes, Richard, *Blake's Songs of Innocence and Experience* (Tate Publishing, 1991)

Hughes, Ted (ed.), *Sylvia Plath: Collected Poems* (Faber and Faber, 1981)

King, Pamela M., *Metaphysical Poets*, York Notes Advanced (York Press, 2001)

'Local Writing Legends', *bbc.co.uk* [website] <www.bbc.co.uk/>

Luminarium: Anthology of English Literature [website] <www.luminarium.org>

McDonald, Trevor, *Favourite Poems* (Michael O'Mara, 1997)

Motion, Andrew, Foreword to *Great poets of the 20th century: Philip Larkin* (Guardian Books, 2008)

Moyle, Franny, *Desperate Romantics: The Private Lives of the Pre-Raphaelites* (John Murray, 2009)

Osborne, Charles (ed.), *The Collins Book of Best-Loved Verse* (Collins, 1986)

Prettejohn, Elizabeth, *The Art of the Pre-Raphaelites* (Tate, 2000)

Ricks, Christoper (ed.), *The Oxford Book of English Verse* (Oxford University Press, 1999)

Schmidt, Michael, *Lives of the Poets* (Weidenfeld & Nicolson, 1998)

Southam, B.C., *A Student's Guide to the Selected Poems of T.S. Eliot* (Faber, 1968)

Stephen, Martin (ed.), *Never Such Innocence: A New Anthology of Great War Verse* (Buchan & Enright, 1988)

Spartacus Educational [website] <www.spartacus.schoolnet.co.uk>

Stevens, Bethan, *Pre-Raphaelites* (The British Museum Press, 2008)

Taggart, Caroline, *I Used To Know That* (Michael O'Mara, 2008)

The Poetry Archive [website] <www.poetryarchive.org>

The Victorian Web [website] <www.victorianweb.org>

Walter, George (ed.), *The Penguin Book of First World War Poetry* (Penguin, 2006)

War Poets Association [website] <www.warpoets.org>

Wikipedia [website] <www.wikipedia.org>

Wilson, A.N., *The Victorians* (Hutchinson, 2002)

Note: there are individual websites for many poets, which are easily found online using a search engine. Only more general websites are listed here, as a lack of space precludes listing all the sites consulted.

ACKNOWLEDGEMENTS

I'd like to thank everyone at Michael O'Mara Books for giving me the opportunity to write this book, especially Alison for her encouragement and Toby for his limitless knowledge, as well as Anna for her help with checking and Glen for his wonderful designs for the cover and text. I'd also like to thank the many friends and colleagues who patiently answered my endless queries and, particularly, my parents for their support and (entirely partial) praise. Finally, I would like to thank Mark for doing the housework around me while I wrote, and for all the coffee.

The author and publishers are grateful to the following for permission to use material that is in copyright:

W. H. Auden: 'Night Mail' and 'Funeral Blues', copyright © 1940, renewed 1968, by W. H. Auden, from *Collected Poems*, ed. Edward Mendelson (Faber and Faber), by permission of Faber and Faber Ltd.

Hilaire Belloc: 'Tarantella', from *Sonnets & Verse* (copyright © Hilaire Belloc 1923), by permission of PFD (www.pfd.co.uk) on behalf of the Estate of Hilaire Belloc.

John Betjeman: 'Slough' and 'A Subaltern's Love Song' from *Collected Poems* (John Murray), copyright © 1955, 1958, 1962, 1964, 1968, 1970, 1979, 1981, 1982, 2001 by John Betjeman, by permission of John Murray (Publishers).

Laurence Binyon: 'For the Fallen' by permission of The Society of Authors as the Literary Representative of the Estate of Laurence Binyon.

Wendy Cope: 'Bloody Men' from *Serious Concerns* (Faber and Faber), copyright © 1992 by Wendy Cope, by permission of Faber and Faber Ltd.

W. H. Davies: 'Leisure' from *The Complete Poems of W. H. Davies* (Jonathan Cape) by permission of Kieron Griffin as Trustee for the Mrs H. M. Davies Will Trust.

INDEX OF POETS

INDEX OF TITLES, FIRST LINES AND FAMILIAR LINES

Titles of poems are in **bold** type, first lines are in roman type, and familiar or well-known lines are in *italic* type following a headword in ***bold italics***.